HOTEL INDUSTRY MANAGEMENT STRATEGY

JOHN LOK

Copyright © John Lok
All Rights Reserved.

This book has been published with all efforts taken to make the material error-free after the consent of the author. However, the author and the publisher do not assume and hereby disclaim any liability to any party for any loss, damage, or disruption caused by errors or omissions, whether such errors or omissions result from negligence, accident, or any other cause.

While every effort has been made to avoid any mistake or omission, this publication is being sold on the condition and understanding that neither the author nor the publishers or printers would be liable in any manner to any person by reason of any mistake or omission in this publication or for any action taken or omitted to be taken or advice rendered or accepted on the basis of this work. For any defect in printing or binding the publishers will be liable only to replace the defective copy by another copy of this work then available.

copyright
2020 Nov. First Print Published
All rights reserved. This book or any portion thereof may not be reproduced or used in any manner whatsoever without the express written permission of the publisher except for the use of brief quotations in a book review or scholarly journal.

Contents

Preface *vii*

Prologue *ix*

1. Hotel Organizational Departments Operation 1
2. Hotel Management Strategy 12
3. Hotel Room Living Service Consumer Psychological Factors 106

Preface

Introduction

Hotel is one kind of booking room living service business. It depends on how many travellers living choice. If it can provide excellent room services to let them to feel comfortable. I believe that the hotel can have good income from travellers. However, any hotels have different design, living room features, entertainment facilities, e.g. restaurants, swimming pools, gym sport etc. different entertainment facilities. Even, on hotel's any facilities can let its travellers to feel similar to another hotel or other hotels facilities. So, in hotel room living service provision market, its competition is very servious.

Due to hotel is one kind of service industy, it is very important to satisfy customer living hotel room and leisure and eating satisfacton. It brings this question: How to implement the hotel's organizational strategy in order to attract travellers to choose to book rooms to live when they are staying in the country? Ought different department supervisor supervise staffs in order to achieve excellent service to satisfy customers needs when they are living in their hotels?

In my this book, I shall explain how different hotel department cooperation in order to achieve efficient strategy in order to raise competition. I hope that my readers can have more clear understanding to learn how hotesl can attempt to achieve effective strategy to raise customers number raising aim more easily.

Prologue

Table of content

Chapter 1
Hotel organizational departments operation p.5-30

Chapter 2
Hotel management strategy
What is hotel management?
How managing a hotel as an independent operator?
Designing hotel website promotion strategy
Hotel Restaurant And Hotel Room Bookings good relationship
strategy
Building good cooperative relationship between travel agents and your hotel in your country
Hotel restaurant food management strategy

Hotel regular reports for effective hotel management strategy

Hotel management software technological strategy
Hotel property facility management strategy
Reputation management strategy

Keys to an effective hotel distribution strategy

The Core Competencies of Hotel Facility Management
Hotel cost / expense control management strategy

Hotel service management strategy

Essential hotel room sales strategies
Hotel promotion strategy
Hotel packages strategy p.31-80
Chapter 3
Hotel room living service consumer psychological factors
What are some noticeable hotel service trends in the industry ?

What's the power of automation for hotels and guests?
Can AI platforms or chatbots raise travellers living hotel room choice need ?
How and why hotel managers need to attempt to predict customer booking hotel room behavior or booking hotel room need psychology? p.81-93
How to supervise teams in hospitality industry
- Behavior modification supervising strategy
- How to design clear job analysis? p.94-119

ONE

HOTEL ORGANIZATIONAL DEPARTMENTS OPERATION

Hotel has different departments, e.g. security deparment, cleaning department, front counter room check in and out department, kitchen cooking department, entertainment facility department, room service department, administration department etc. However, any departments must be very important to influence whole organizational performance. It does not depend on which department is especial important to influence whole organizational service performance. For example, room service department main function is let room living customers to feel comfortable to live in any big, small , middle size hotel rooms. If any one hotel room can not let the customer feels comfortable to live or it is dirty to live. Then, it will bring poor living service performance to cause the customer does not choose to live the hotel to live again. However, it does not mean that room service department must be the most important department in whole hotel organization because all hotel department individual performance and efficiency will influence whole hotel operational efficiency to let all customers to feel. I shall explain all hotel organizations departmental operations as below:

In order to run the Hotel as a functional unit, there are several departments in a hotel which work and coordinate together and the major departments of the hotel are:

1. Front Office Department
2. Housekeeping Department
3. Food and Beverage Service Department
4. Kitchen or Food Production Department
5. Engineering and Maintenance Department
6. Accounts and Credits Department
7. Security Department
8. Human Resources (HR) Department
9. Sales and Marketing Department
10. Purchase Department
11. Information Technology (IT)

1. Front Office Department:

Every day is different with the arrival of new personalities from different walks of life. The Front Office Department is often referred as the nerve centre of the hotel as it is in constant contact with our guests, and has the most diverse operating exposure. Our team is passionate about guest service and look at every possible opportunity to make our guests comfortable during their stay. Our front office associates have a keen intuition that allows them to anticipate our guest's needs and exceed them. With its excellent communication skills, it is not unusual for our staff to multi task and work diligently in order to resolve any issues that may arise.

This department performs various functions like reservation, reception, registration, room assignment, and settlement of bills of a resident guest and the front office department is considered as the nerve centre of a hotel.The front-office staff welcome the guests, carry their luggage, help them register, give them their room keys and mail, answer questions about the activities in the hotel and surrounding area, and finally check them out. In fact, the only direct contact most guests have with hotel employees, other than in the restaurants, is with members of the front-office staff.

Concierge is extra service department – Always At Your Service, concierge is constantly looking for ways to enhance your guest experience. Travel routes, recommendations of tours, attractions, and short cuts around town are just a few services offered by our remarkable Concierge Team, topped by, of course, a lovely friendly welcome!

2. Housekeeping Department:

Every morning is a busy one in the Housekeeping Department. The team has an eminent eye for attention to detail to provide our guests with a spotless guest experience. Our housekeepers are in charge of almost every detail of your stay from the fluffy pillows and sheets in your guest rooms to the replenishment of your bathroom amenities. The Housekeeping Department is a critical function to the hotel's continued success!

The housekeeping department is responsible for the cleanliness, maintenance, and aesthetic upkeep of rooms, public areas, back areas, and surroundings in a hotel and for the immaculate care and upkeep of all guest rooms and public spaces at all times.The staff members who excel in the Housekeeping Departments have an eye for detail and a commitment to the training, development and motivation of a diverse group of talented employees. It is the service and cleanliness that really make an impact on our guests and determine whether they will return and also recommend the hotel to others.

3. Food and Beverage Service Department:

The hotel lounge restaurant are a vibrant bunch with a combination of proficiency and bubbly personalities. Whether it's for breakfast, lunch, dinner cocktails or appetizers, our team will always serve you with a smile.This department looks after the service of food and drinks to guests. The Food which is made in the Kitchen and Drinks prepared in the Bar to the Customers (Guest) at the Food & Beverage premises. Some examples of the food and beverage outlets are Restaurants, Bars, Hotels, Airlines, Cruise Ships, Trains, Companies, Schools, Colleges, Hospitals, Prisons, Takeaway etc.

4. Kitchen or Food Production Department:

An experienced team of chefs offers a great variety of scrumptious dishes to keep our hungry customers happy. Although our chefs work in a fast paced environment, the kitchen is far from what you see on Reality TV! There is a less drama and more fun as our chefs handle the line with their experience, great personalities and talent.All the food and beverages that are served to the hotel guest is prepared in the kitchen. Culinary preparation, as an art and science in the modern kitchen, required more than just a knowledge of food being prepared and the methods of preparation.It is through a knowledge of basic skills, terminology, and rules of the kitchen that a final goal, preparation and service of quality is achieved in the hotel kitchen.

5. Engineering and Maintenance Department:

Running an effective hotel requires careful planning and hard work. Equipment does break down; meaning repairs and regular preventive maintenance are required around the hotel. Our professional Maintenance Team performs a wide range of essential tasks to help ensure a smooth operation resulting in happy guests.

The engineering department is responsible for repairing and maintaining the plant and machinery, water treatment and distribution, boilers and water heating, sewage treatment, external and common area lighting, fountains and water features etc. Also, It looks after the maintenance of all the equipment, furniture and fixture installed in a hotel.

6. Accounts and Credits Department:

The Accounting Team plays a significant role in the managing of hotel expense control aspect. They provide the hotel with relevant financial data and forecasts which are used for daily decision making to ensure we are thriving and keeping the books up to date. The team offers a great support service to all departments with financial recommendations.

This department maintains all the financial transactions. Accounting departments typically handle a variety of important tasks. Such tasks often include invoicing customers, accounts receivable monitoring and collections, account reconciliations, payables processing, consolidation of multiple entities under common ownership, budgeting, periodic financial reporting as well as financial analysis. Also common are setting up adequate internal controls for all business processes (to prevent theft/misappropriation of assets), handling external audits and dealing with banks in order to obtain financing. Taxes are sometimes handled by accounting departments in house, but this work is often contracted to outside tax accountants.

7. Security Department:

The security department of a hotel is responsible for the overall security of the hotel building, in-house guests, visitors, day users, and employees of the hotel, and also their belongings.

8. H R and Admin department:

The Executive Team plays a decisive role in the hotel operations as the final decision-maker. The team is comprised of the Department Heads and is led by the Director of Operations, and the General Manager. The team ensures the smooth running of hotel operations, each member responsible for the management of its own department. Regular meetings are organized to discuss any issues and find ways to continuously improve business profitability and guest experience.

Human Resource department is responsible for the acquisition, utilisation, training, and development of the human resources of the hotel.The role of the HR department also has to do with the administration of an impartial and internal justice system which will promote transparency and openness in organisational communication. The Human resources department also serves as a progressive voice in a common system and strives to ensure competitiveness in the conditions of service for staff.

9. Sales and Marketing Department:

Sales Team works hard to promote the brand and the amenities of the hotel. The Sales Department is in charge of negotiating and prospecting large business and leisure groups, tours operators and individual travellers. The

Marketing Department is the analytical backbone of Sales as well as being responsible for increasing exposure for the hotel through various advertising opportunities both in print and on the Web. Be sure to engage with us on our various social media platforms such as, Facebook, Twitter, Google Plus, or Pinterest! The major role of the sales and marketing department is to bring in business and also to increase the sales of the hotel's products and services is the major task of the department.

In addition, catering Department is responsible for the smooth operation and sales of our beautifully appointed conference centre. From corporate meetings to large celebratory events, the catering team must to take ownership of every detail with excellent teamwork and efficient communication in order to meet and exceed the expectations of our clients.

10. Purchase Department:

The purchase department is responsible for procuring the inventories of all the departments of a hotel.

11. Information Technology (IT) / Systems

The Information Technology department is responsible for the day-to-day support of all IT systems, business systems, office systems, computer networks, and telephony systems throughout the hotel/resort. Additionally responsible for Information Technology issues, products, and services at the property. Provides user training and support of all property/site systems, network enhancements, hardware and software support etc.

Above all of different departments are very important to influence any hotel organization's efficiency and service performance. They are inter-connective to influence any service aspects to let any customer to feel whether the hotel overall performance can satisfy his/her living need. For example, if the hotel's front office service performance is poor, this department service staff can not book any rooms vancancy to let any one customer to live when he/she arrives this hotel to check in immediately. Then, many customers will not live the hotel room when he/she walk in to the hotel to prepare book room immediately , then it cause many customers only choose another hotel to live. So, any hotels must need to plan enough big, middle and small size rooms to prepare any customers can live their rooms immediately.

So, front office's room booking budget plan can influence whole hotel customer number.Even, if the hotel's room clearning service can not satisfy any customers feel comfortable to live when they live in dirty room, or any rooms' bath room and sleeping room are dirty, then it will cause any customers won't choose to live this hotel when they travel to this country again, they can choose any one hotel to replace this poor room living service performance hotel significantly. So, it seems that any one hotel department individual performance must influence all customer individual satisfactory level. When the customer feels the hotel can not provide excellent service and/or room living satisfaction to let he/she feels, they the hotel will lose many customers from this kind intangible customer feeling factor easily. Hence, how to implement effective strategy to let customers to feel satisfactory when they choose to live the hotel, it is one important value question to research.

However, I feel that these seven key aspects, any hotel organizations need to consider in order to achieve service efficient raising and provide excellent room living service to let any one customer to feel, they may include as below:

A hotel wouldn't run smoothly without the right people and

right resources in the right departments. If you're new to the hotel business, or just doing your fair share of basic research, read below for the outline of a hotel's structure. Your exact needs may not be the same as other hotels, which can be affected by the size of your establishment, whether you offer full service or not, and what amenities you have. But most hotels have the following seven areas in common. These areas reflect the various job roles that will need to be filled to keep the organization running. Being aware of these departments can help you plan for future success.

On Executives Service Aspect

These are the decision makers within the business. They may be department heads, managers, or directors. Depending on how your company runs and the size of it, executives may be responsible for some of the other areas discussed below, including accounting, marketing, and at times even front desk services.

On Front Desk Services Aspect

Although no operational segment within a hotel organization is dispensable, it could be argued that very little would happen without the front office staff. These people are constantly in contact with guests, and may even be responsible for taking and handling bookings. Detail-oriented people are often required for this role, since they must meet the exact needs of the guests. Sometimes concierge may also be lumped in with this division of the business, but could be an entirely different department worth building.

On Housekeeping Services Aspect

Keeping your guest rooms clean and tidy is an essential task. Your housekeeping team is typically responsible for every detail within a room, from the cleanliness of the sheets to keeping toiletries stocked.

On Maintenance Facility Management Aspect

Even the best quality utilities and electronics can break and malfunction. In today's tech-oriented world, there is also more to repair and fix in terms of computers, TV screens, game consoles, DVD players, and other cutting-edge tech items than before. Tech can sometimes also be the responsibility of executives or front desk services, depending on what works best for the organization. Additionally, in some cases, maintenance might be lumped in with housekeeping or another role. Again, it depends on the size of your business and the personnel available to you.

On Accounting Administration Management Aspect

Every business needs proper accounting. Tracking expenses and revenue helps you keep a finger on the pulse of the business, so you can make tweaks and adjustments as necessary. The accounting team is usually directly answerable to the executive team, providing them with relevant data and forecasts. They may also make recommendations and offer support for other departments.

On Marketing & Sales Strategy Aspect

Every business requires promotion. The marketing team is responsible for converting prospects into paying guests and spreading the brand message. They must keep up-to-date with the latest marketing channels and practices, including social media, content marketing, OTAs, and so on. Marketing can sometimes become the responsibility of front desk services. But because executives often want control over the exact message that's being shared with their target audience, they will sometimes take it on – especially if they don't have a pre-existing marketing department. Plus, to entrepreneurs, business development is often the most exciting part.

On Managing Kitchen Staff Task Aspect

If you're a full-service hotel, if you offer room service, or both, then it's impossible to keep up with orders and meet your guest's dining needs without competent kitchen staff. Some hotels also need a separate catering team, especially for conference rooms.

When, having the right structure in place is critical to the success of your organization overall. Finding the right balance can be challenging, because human resource is often the most expensive resource of all. At the same time, they are also your greatest resource, and your hotel must cultivate and utilize them well.

All of above deparments are any hotel essential departments in their organizational structure. Any one department's efficiency and function and operation must may influence another department or other departments operation efficienctly. For example, if the cleaning room bed supplied matieral department cleaning staffs efficiencies are low, then, their efficiencies can influence any hotel rooms bed matieral, toilet towel , toilet teeth paste, toilet paper room cleaning supplies have enough supply. So, this deparment has close relationship to influence any hotel rooms have enough clean toilet and hotel room daily materials supplies. Consequently, any it will cause many customers feel hotel rooms' any bed, toilet daily supplies are not enough to be supplied clean hotel bed, toilet daily tools. So, any hotels need to consider how to adjust any department individual operational efficiency absolutely in order to avoid any hotel customers feel poor service performance to your hotel.

TWO

HOTEL MANAGEMENT STRATEGY

- What is hotel management?

Hotel management is really about overseeing every operation of the property. This requires knowledge of distribution strategy, finance, customer service, staff management, marketing, and more. In no way should any of these be treated as 'set and forget'. Hotel management is about constantly evaluating performance is every facet of the business and making necessary adjustments.

Ultimately effective hotel management will not only ensure your hotel stays in business, but is able to profit and grow over time. Think of the hotel as an ecosystem that will get healthier the better you manage it. As your hotel becomes more successful you can upgrade and charge higher rates, pay staff higher wages, and create an experience that guests want to come back for. It can take time to get everything right however. There are many skills you'll already possess but many others you need to learn along the way, or else hire staff that can provide the knowledge for you.

Hotel management definition

Definition of hotel management is that it's 'a field of business and a study, that tends itself to the operational aspects of a hotel as well as a wide range of affiliated topics. Such as: Accounting, administration, finance, information systems, human resource management, public relations, strategy, marketing, revenue management, sales, change management, leadership, gastronomy and more.'Clearly there's a lot to be aware of and many of these functions do require specialists. However not all properties have the luxury of hiring a full team of staff, so it's certainly not impossible to run a successful small hotel business without a range of degrees.

What does hotel management strategy mean? Hotel management strategy may include: service performance management, facility management, cost or expense control management three aspects. Service performance management main aims to let customers to feel the hotel's security is safe when they are living in the hotel, front office service, room service room, even, restaurant food delivery service, entertainment service, such as swimming, gym sport , tennis sport etc. different kinds of whole service can let customers to feel satisfactory as well as facility management service, e.g. swimming pools can let swimmers to feel safe when they are swimming, swimming pools water is warm and clean when they are swimming, swimming pools facility is new, or sport gym running machine, riding machine facility is safe to use and new sport facility can let them to feel to play when they use any kinds of sport tools facility, the hotel room's kitchen tools are clearn, enough provison, kitchen is clean, room is clean, e.g. beds, toilets, drinking cups, plates are clean and enough number provision, when fire occurrence, the stairs areas are large sizes to let many people run on the hotel staires when many customers are running down in the same time. All of any hotel facilities will let customers feel safe or new use in order to let them to feel comfortable to live in the hotel as well as control cost is the main aspect to assist the hotel how to avoid to expend excess expenditure per month. So, how to implement cost control strategy will influence any one hotel income. All of these three aspects may be any one hotel main considerable issues. How to implement effective strategies will be one important discussion issue as below:

Hotel facility management strategy

For hoteliers, hotel management is not one concept. It's hard to really say you've mastered hotel management when it comes with such a range of roles and responsibilities. Being able to adapt, meet challenges, and place yourself on a scale of personal growth is vital for a hotel manager.

There are always new strategies, traveller preferences, or industry technologies emerging that you have to keep track of. Even new roles within hotels and the hotel industry are being created that will affect the way one manages their property.This blog will take you through the major considerations to keep in mind regarding hotel management and throw some tips and ideas along the way, to help you run a better hotel business.

● How managing a hotel as an independent operator?

Hotel operations management: Inventory and revenue

The day to day operations of a hotel are pretty all encompassing. Is everything that guests need in order? Are staff and cleaning schedules organised? Is the occupancy rate where you'd like it to be? Obviously a core aspect of

hotel management is to manage your rooms; or your inventory.
Effective inventory management for hotels involves both creating and managing demand, and maximising returns. The investment backing a hotel is tied up in its rooms and the returns can only be gained from selling those rooms optimally.

Here are some strategy basics:

1. Pricing strategy

By driving prices up during high peak periods and knowing how much to discount prices by to ensure rooms are rented during low peak periods, hotels can maximise their return. Through dynamic pricing, businesses can provide discounts and incentives in a controlled way during different seasons.

2. Distribution strategy

Hotels generally advertise their rooms through multiple channels, such as online travel agencies, to optimise reach and promote sales. Distribution management is essential and this involves calculating the minimum numbers of rooms needing to be sold for any given period by each channel. In doing so, you then have the ability to make informed choices regarding reallocation from cancellations or where to list spare rooms to maximise sales.

3. Market segmentation

Being aware of your hotel room visitor need market and the variable preferences, demands and affordability of different demographics are paramount to understanding how to price and distribute your room sales across the various channels. Not only does this help in managing your existing rooms, but it can also allow you to capture more of the market and increase sales and revenue. Flexibility is an important virtue required of hoteliers and being able to understand your clientele and adapt to their needs is vital to building loyalty and guaranteeing profitability.

Revenue management is another huge part of managing your hotel. How do your hotel get smore money coming in and achieve business goals? Smart revenue management and pricing strategies are needed if you want to optimise your Average Daily Rate . I shall recommend some hotel promotion methods as below:

1. Packages, promotions and extras

Packages are any rate that pairs the accommodation with an add-on; it could be free breakfast, free parking, or a ticket to a local event or attraction.Take a look at these methods to make sure your packages offer a unique experience.

Promotions are special rates that can change depending on:

The season or holiday period;

If the guest is a VIP; or,

You want to capitalise on an event.

You can get even more specific by offering things like mobile-only promotions.

Extras are an added expenditure that guests will only realise they want during the booking process. This might include items like champagne and chocolate stocked in their room, shuttle services from the airport, or activities like exercise classes. Extras are an added expenditure that guests will only realise they want during the booking process. This might include items like champagne and chocolate stocked in their room, shuttle services from the airport, or activities like exercise classes.

2. Events and tours

Selling tickets to local events, tours, or offering car rental is a good point-of-sale opportunity to increase your revenue per customer as well as providing a more satisfying experience for your guest.

3. Sell your hotel products

If you offer your guests the chance to buy your shampoo, bath and beach towels, art pieces, linen and so on, it can provide you with extra revenue and might even save you from the cost of replacing items that guests 'accidentally' pack with their own luggage when they depart.

4. Referrals and return business

If your guests give you positive feedback on completion of their stay, encourage them to share their experience with family and friends, and on social media to drive more bookings and brand awareness. You could also set guests up with a promotion code to get a discount the next time they stay. This encourages return business and helps you keep a consistent occupancy rate.

5. Accommodate flexible travellers

Some travellers don't have a set itinerary or allow themselves flexibility with their schedule, so take the opportunity to raise your occupancy and incremental revenue by offering guests a discount for an additional night's stay. Some mistakes have worse consequences than others and depending on the industry, backlash can range from minor to cataclysmic. The type of mistake you make will also have an impact on this. Did it just affect you, or did it also affect your customers?

- Designing hotel website promotion strategy

However, in the hospitality industry almost everything revolves around the customer, and they're the quickest party to point out any flaws. There's also plenty of times where you might simply self-sabotage and fail to get the most out of your business. Human fallibility prevents us from eliminating all our mistakes, but you can certainly look out for some common errors to avoid. I shall indicate some human avoidance mistakes on hotel website design and advertment skillful aspect to cause poor hotel room customer individual experience from your hotel website advertisement as below:

1. Failing to provide basic contact information

A beautiful looking hotel website with a fancy design and stunning features means nothing to the customer if they can't find your address or phone number on the homepage. The basics are something every hotel must get right before anything else. Travellers have all kinds of queries and many of them want to call to get instant clarification, and often people will be calling to make a booking so your phone number is an absolutely essential piece of information.

2. Website scarecrows – autoplay videos and music

Many people book holidays between the hours of 9AM – 5PM, i.e work hours. The last thing they need is for their computer to start blasting commercials or ditties around the office. The first thing they'll do is close your website and it's unlikely they'll return.

3. Incorrect use of social media

It's great to use social media as a marketing avenue but it's important you use it in the right way. You want traffic to be directed to your website and booking pages, not away from them. A common mistake hoteliers make is sending website visitors away to their social media channels immediately after a visitor has landed on the homepage. How many people are going to be coming back once they've been redirected to YouTube for instance?

4. Poor quality photos

There's really no point in investing in a great website design if the photos you integrate into the theme are lacking quality. Travellers want to see what they're paying for and if what they see is a grainy, blurry, or poorly framed image they won't be racing to open their wallets. Paying for high quality photography is worth every penny and you should update your images every couple of years, or every time you refurbish.

5. Downloads for simple information

Does anyone actually enjoy downloading a PDF to their phone or computer? The answer is probably no so why would you make a prospective guest do this? If a traveller wants to view the menu of your hotel restaurant for example, they should be able to do it on your website. Making them download documents is a conversion killer.

6. Connecting to the wrong distribution channels

When you connect to online travel agents manually or via a channel manager, it's still important to do some research. You have to look beyond the four or five biggest channels and find partners that most suit your target market.

7. Ignoring the potential of the local area

Guests are simply buying a hotel room when they come to stay at your hotel. For them, they're paying for an experience delivered by the destination. It would be silly for you not to take advantage of this. Make sure you partner with local businesses and run promotions and packages around local events and attractions.

8. Closing your ears (and mouth) to feedback

Reviews are one of the most important aspects to get right for your hotel. Customer satisfaction and brand reputation are vital if you want to keep the bookings coming in. The worst thing you can do is stay silent online when people leave reviews and feedback on sites like TripAdvisor or your social media pages. You need to respond diligently to both positive and negative reviews.

9. Not paying close attention to seasonality

The price people are prepared to pay for their hotel room will depend on the supply and demand trends over time. Seasonality matters, and you'll have to change rates a number of times during the year to reflect buying behavior and market conditions. This, together with the date and timing release of packages and promotions forms an integral part of your sales and marketing plan.

10. Lacking attention to detail in housekeeping

One of the most common complaints from guests is about dirty rooms or general uncleanliness of the hotel. There should never be any shortcutting when it comes to housekeeping and cleaning. Not only is it a healthy and safety issue, but you open yourself up to a flood of negative reviews. Of course, there are plenty of other pitfalls that could hit your hotel so you have to be constantly diligent and find ways to optimise your processes, reducing the risk of mistakes that could cost you money.

● Hotel and restaurant management strategy

Life gets even more complicated for hotels that also have a restaurant. Since managing a restaurant is a whole other kettle of fish. A study by Leonardo looked at what images travel shoppers viewed the most. Obviously the number one result was guest rooms but the second most viewed was restaurant photos.

This indicates that travel boils down to two primary needs; people want a nice place to sleep and they want a nice place to eat. Most of the time the hotel restaurant is a solid driver of revenue and an integral part of the hotel's identity, so it's ability to help market and sell your hotel should not be underestimated. Here are some reasons your restaurant will drive more bookings and how you can aid the process:

1. Individualise your restaurant

The first thing you need to do is to maximise the quality of your product by treating your hotel restaurant as a restaurant in its own right, rather than a glorified bar only accessible by guests. Turn your restaurant into a premium dining experience that focuses on the whole package including the food, lighting, music, decor, and wine lists. This way, your restaurant won't only be the bait to bring new customers in, but also an incentive for current guests to return when they revisit the area. At the same time it's important to remember who your customers are and understand what they want and what they can afford. Create a menu that will sell, not one you think is cool and trendy, and make sure the pricing is in alignment with the rest of your hotel. Using local produce will help with this.

2. Give your restaurant its own website

Don't let the physical setting of your restaurant deter you from creating a separate website for it. While it should also be featured on your hotel website, a dedicated restaurant website will help maximise revenue and potentially increase traffic to your hotel via page links.The restaurant website should feature large, high-resolution images and videos to showcase the food and decor. Hopefully, if guests land here and see they can also stay in the hotel, they'll be more convinced to stay and book direct.

By cross-referencing both lines of business you'll improve your search engine optimisation and maximise the traffic and conversions you receive. You should make sure everything is optimised for mobile devices and you could also include a direct link to your hotel's booking engine on your restaurant website.

By dedicating a separate website to your restaurant you'll be catering to consumer's need for relevant and distinctive content while also increasing your web presence. It's definitely worth the time and effort, especially if you use a smart intuitive website builder.

3. Make offers or give discounts

Consider offering different restaurant deals for different parts of the week to further encourage people to book with your hotel. Midweek you might advertise via social media or another medium giving away cheaper drinks or free desserts. On the weekend you might include a discounted three-course meal with a booking. As we know, managing a hotel is an extremely complex, stressful, and time-consuming task. The same can be said of running a successful restaurant. Combining both might seem like a fool's errand. And while there's definitely some risks involved in such an enterprise, there's also the opportunity for rich rewards at your hotel.

Hotel restaurant management: How you need to operate

Not only does a successful hotel restaurant have to serve and please your guests at your property, it has to stand on its own as a dining option for anyone in the local area. This is because many guests will want to explore the city and the many options available to them. So if you can't convince your guests to stay in for a meal, you have to attract other paying patrons. Who knows, some diners might even decide to make it a night and book a room directly through your front desk. For this to work the quality of your product has to be high. Your hotel restaurant has to individualise itself and offer a comprehensive dining experience. This means in addition to great food, you need to focus on lighting, music, decor and well thought out wine lists.

Things you need to consider include:

1. Hotel Space

How big will your restaurant attraction be relative to your

hotel?
Different departments Staff number
How many patrons can you serve and how many extra staff will you need to oversee this?

2. Restaurent Food Menu

Will you create a menu that sells and is affordable or one that is cool and trendy? Make sure it's in line with who you expect to enter your restaurant.

3. Hotel Room And Food Packages

Obviously giving guests deals and discounts when they book a room direct with you will help increase restaurant traffic and revenue for your property.

- Hotel Restaurant And Hotel Room Bookings good relationship strategy

You should always reserve some tables for your own customers. If a guest walks down to eat and the restaurant is booked out by people not staying at the hotel, the response may be less than favourable.
The main issue is that if your restaurant is receiving poor reviews, it could be turning people off booking a room, no matter how amazing the rest of your hotel is. If it looks like the effort to produce the best possible experience is missing in the restaurant, travellers will assume the same for your whole business and look elsewhere. The same risk applies on the other side of the coin. If your hotel is derided for a poor experience and your occupancy is low, your restaurant could dwindle and die if it relies solely on business from outside the hotel walls.

Your hotel and restaurant have to work in harmony to keep each other strong.

Here are five tips to make your hotel restaurant a success:

1. Strike a balance between class and convenience

For guests already staying at your hotel your restaurant should be a quick and easy place to get a meal. They won't want to spend too much money, nor spend too much time waiting for food if they have other plans. On the other hand, diners coming for the restaurant alone will be expecting first-class ambience, food, and service.To keep everyone hotel customer feels happy and satisfactory when they are living in your hotel, you need to offer a simple but delicious menu that can be eaten in a comfortable setting that also promotes social interaction.

2. Give your restaurant its own website

While it should certainly be featured on your hotel website, a dedicated restaurant website will help maximise revenue and potentially drive extra traffic through your hotel via links. Cross-referencing both lines of business will improve your SEO and help maximise conversions and direct bookings. On your restaurant website, feature large high-resolution images and videos to showcase your food and decor. It will bring attractive and exciting website photos to persuade your potential hotel customers to choose to live your hotel.

3. Create a social media page for your restaurant

If your hotel restaurant has its own website it stands to reason it should have its own Facebook page too. This is especially true if regular events are hosted. Think live music on Friday nights, monthly wine tasting, or happy hours. It's also useful for posting pictures of your food and dining experience.

4. Offer deals and discounts

You can use different parts of the week and different mediums to drive customers to your restaurant. Before a guest arrives, email them a drink voucher for the restaurant bar. It's likely they'll also grab a meal. You might use social media midweek to promote cheaper drinks or free desserts with every meal order. On the weekend, you could offer a three-course deal when a guest makes a booking.

5. Hire talented hospitality staff

Given the unique challenge of running a restaurant, you need staff that are specifically trained to meet it. Give them the power to create the best possible restaurant experience for your hotel's guests. Hotels and restaurants both form a large part of the hospitality industry and customer service is vital to both. These businesses live and die by customer satisfaction because of the public exposure they're always open to. Guests are only too eager to share stories of their holiday or dining experience – both good and bad.

- Building good cooperative relationship between travel agents and your hotel in your country

Hotel management: Optimising your online travel agent profile. It's common knowledge hotels are at a disadvantage if they aren't engaging online travel agents to boost their distribution and sell rooms. The prominence of OTAs, such as Expedia and Booking.com, continues to grow and they're a proven resource for travellers who use them to discover a diverse range of accommodation options at the best price. Connecting to OTAs will help hotels increase visibility and maintain their occupancy. Your property may even rank higher on search engines – and yet the commission fee from OTAs can feel like a necessary evil if hotels want to accomplish this. However, to make sure you get the full benefit of OTAs and their reach, there's a number of steps you should follow to optimise your hotel's profile. Given your hotel is a brand, your marketing efforts should be consistent across all channels. Don't save your best images and content just for your website, make sure this is also on the OTA websites.

Similar to search engines such as Google, OTAs have their own algorithms for how your property will rank, meaning you need to pay close attention to the following tips:

Here are 6 easy steps to optimise your hotel's OTA profile:

1. Accurately manage your inventory

Because the availability of your rooms will fluctuate due to peak periods or seasonal changes, you need to maintain an accurate inventory across all OTAs to keep your occupancy rate high. Using a channel manager with pooled inventory is the best way to achieve this because travellers won't be disrupted by double booking issues or incorrect data.

2. Cleverly manage your rates and promotions

Guests don't simply use OTAs for a wide range of choice and inspiration, often they're looking for last minute deals and offers. If you have time-sensitive promotions they'll have more chance of being caught and you can more easily sell the remainder of your rooms. It's not hard to make alterations on OTAs to highlight a particular rate or capitalise on seasonal events to attract more guests to your property profile.

3. Carefully respond to reviews

While only 14% of consumers trust traditional advertising, 92% respect reviews on sites such as TripAdvisor. Reviews on OTAs are traditionally reliable because guests can only post a review after they've stayed at the property. However, only 36% of hoteliers respond to reviews on OTA sites. It's important to do an efficient job of managing online reviews.

4. Consider paid advertising

This doesn't have to be restricted to big and rich hotel

corporations. It can also be a viable option for independent hotels on a pay-per-click basis. While paid advertising is no guarantee of more bookings, it will help make your property front-of-mind. If your content and aesthetic is strong enough, you should see a rise in revenue and your OTA ranking.

5. Focus on specific markets

Narrowing down your targets will mean you impact a lower volume of customers but you're also more likely to secure the bookings you want if you use certain time periods, events, geo-targeting or other methods to target specific audiences.

6. Understand your competition

It's vital to know who the similar players in your market are so you aren't significantly underselling or overselling your rooms. If you are, you won't be able to compete. On top of this, being aware of their activity may provide an opportunity to snare extra bookings. For example, changing rates could indicate the occupancy of a competitor or a promotion based on something you could also benefit from. There are specific data systems hotels can use to monitor competitors. With an optimised OTA profile, your hotel will not only gain bookings from third-party channels but direct traffic to your website should also increase, helping you to offset the commission fee you pay.

- Hotel restaurant food management strategy

To improve the way you manage your hotel, you have to think about everything and look for ways to save time and money, or increase efficiency. Even small changes can reap big rewards over the course of a financial year. Sticking with the theme of food, there's a big opportunity here. As humans, food represents our most essential connection to the planet and its resources. Yet environmental researchers often surmise that we place less value on food than we used to. Following US hotel kitchen indicates that hotel GDP information. You only have to look at numbers from Hotel Kitchen around food waste to understand their perspective:

In the US alone, an estimated 40% of all food is scrapped
American hotels serve food worth $35 billion each year
It's estimated that 40% of food in customer-facing businesses, such as hotels and supermarkets, goes to waste

How to control food waste in your hotel's kitchen
Fighting food waste at your hotel goes beyond feeding people and helping the environment – it also improves your property's bottom line. Do you really know how much food you throw away each week? Have you worked out its monetary value? Are staff and guests aware of your efforts to be more sustainable and properly manage food waste disposal? According to Hotel Kitchen, more than 90% of staff say they want to take action on tackling food waste. Guests are also becoming increasingly savvy with 60% of those surveyed saying they expect hotels to be actively reducing waste across their operations.

There may be steps your hotel restaurant can take to reduce waste:

1. Get buy in on food waste from your team
Create a team to take ownership of waste reduction and incentivise them. This should include a cook or chef and a kitchen porter (KP). Your KPs see what gets scraped off plates, while a chef will know how leftover ingredients can be better used in future menus.

2. Research waste management software to support processes
Conduct a waste audit, by dividing waste into categories and ensuring staff dispose of it in an appropriately-labelled container. There is weight-based software for this: basically

a talking bin that records the weight of different categories of waste according to descriptions entered by staff on a touchscreen. The most well-known of these is probably the Winnow system, which its manufacturer claims typically saves operators 3-5% on food costs – a ROI of up to 10 times within a year. The challenges with using a system like this is that, it requires all waste to go into the same bin, leading to congestion in the kitchen or pot wash, and it can take time to input the data.

3. Assess raw ingredients vs. diners' plates

If conducting a waste audit manually, you'll need to at least split waste into raw ingredients and prepared waste that is left on diners' plates. Almost 10% of raw ingredients are wasted. This includes things like potato peelings and cauliflower leaves, which can be difficult to find a use for. Raw ingredients also covers kitchen prep mistakes. Some 35% of restaurant waste is left on diners' plates. This is most definitely higher in a hotel restaurant, where diners are less likely to take their leftovers home.

4. Asking staff for their frequent observations

Raw ingredients and diners' plates might be the two main categories, but make sure you have as many containers as you have space for. Record the waste, by weight, but also anecdotally. You'll learn more from staff comments: what did they find surprising? Was there an item plated but not eaten? Is there a garnish that customers commonly leave?

5. Following the 'less is more' approach

Assemble as many staff as possible to discuss the results, after a fortnight or a month. When it comes to prepared waste, you may find that it's a result of portion sizes being too large, in which case introduce strict portion controls, possibly using measure scoops that are colour-coded for different items. If lots of butter and preserve is left after breakfast service, consider buying in individual wrapped portions. Keep in mind that, unavoidable post-consumer waste can often be used by farmers as animal feed: all good content for your Instagram stories.

6. Obsessing over food and beverage expiration dates

If you discover that fresh items are going out of date, introduce a strict fridge rotation system and coloured stickers to identify which items to use first. Store new foods on the right fridge and existing on the left to maximise shelf life. Get this ingrained and replicate it in ambient storage areas for rice, herbs and spices, pulses and grains as well. Out of date ingredients can usually be donated to local food banks. Build a relationship with your local food bank operator and post about it on social media to boost your presence in the local community. This may lead to worthwhile involvement in charity events.

7. Sharpen up your kitchen team's knife skills

Meat carcasses should always be used for stock. If staff report that there is still a lot of meat left on bones, check that knives are being properly sharpened and that staff are trained to bone items efficiently. If staff lack butchery and fishmongers skills you'll save on waste by buying, for example, cubed chicken and filleted fish.

8. Using proper peelers for vegetables

Similarly, are staff prepping vegetables properly? You'll see less waste using peelers than knives for most fruit and root vegetables.

9. Allocating some space for composting

Raw vegetable waste can be composted if you have some outside space. A compost area can be simply constructed out of pallets. The resulting compost can be used to improve the soil on site or donated to local allotment groups. It can often be valuable to look at what businesses in other parts of your industry are doing, and seeing how you compare or what you might be able to employ in your own business strategies.

10. Getting customer service ideas from restaurants

There are similarities between service in restaurants and hotels, but also a few differences. Let's see how great customer service in restaurants translates to achieving guest satisfaction in hotels.

A great first step is turning 'service' into 'hospitality'

Service is basically about performing a task; doing something for someone. It denotes a mechanical action. On the other hand, hospitality is about making an impression on someone and going the extra mile to make their experience a memorable one. The interaction involved in hospitality is a genuine one and should be based on a caring attitude. Hospitality is something the best restaurants do extremely well. Customers will generally be served by one waiter their entire visit and will be made to feel like close friends or family, constantly attended to and conversed with warmly. Any requests will be responded to immediately. By the end of the meal, customers will look forward to coming back and seeing their waiter again.

In hotels, guests might interact with many different staff members throughout their stay, meaning they don't always get this personal connection. They may have to wait longer for services and might get frustrated when the staff member doesn't remember their preferences. The attentiveness of restaurants is certainly something hotels can try to replicate. Some things to try is to greet guests by name, get to know their interests, and don't delay when they want attention.

Giving guests a personalised experience at your hotel

A recent report shows full-service and fast food restaurants are revamping their menus and establishing more mobile ordering options, to the delight of customers. Restaurants are adapting their menus and technology to align with shifting consumer preferences. This looks at millennial tastes for fresh food, mobile ordering, and automated kiosks. The bottom line is that restaurants are working hard to please consumers in a way the customers are dictating, resulting in higher satisfaction.

Hotels need to do the same. New technology, both front and backend, needs to be explored if customer service is to improve. Again this comes back to hospitality and personalisation. Give each specific guest what they need. Even if you look at mobile check-in, it's not something everyone wants. Obviously some guests will be in a rush or tired from travel and simply want to get to their room as fast as possible. Others will be craving some human interaction. It's about what's convenient for the individual hotel guest. Technology should be able to help hotels in every regard. Think about how technology can improve the in-room experience, especially when it comes to speeding up room service or cleaning processes. Conversely, if backend tech that makes it easier to manage reservations and distribution is used, more time can be dedicated to guest experience.

Empower staff to solve their own problems

Nothing will frustrate a customer more than a staff member always needing to clear something with their manager. Not only does this take more time, but it makes the staff member look incompetent. Quality restaurants will take difficult or specific requests in their stride and provide customers with any special needs they require. If something goes wrong, their constant hands-on experience allows them to solve it, without the intervention of a manager. Again, it's done with a smile on their face because nothing is too much trouble for a valued customer.

Hotels need to train and empower their staff this way too. A great example is The Ritz-Carlton Hotel Company, where even hourly employees have permission to spend up to $2,000 per guest to solve any problem or dissatisfaction that may arise, without needing to ask for approval or involve management. And it's not the amount of money that's the point; it's the instant no-need-for-approval empowerment, which enables quick solutions for guests.

Hire the right traits in staff at your hotel

The very best restaurant staff show a passion for their job and authentic desire to make people happy. While the hospitality industry is one where skills can be learned on the job and thus standards may be lax, the approach taken to hiring staff must be taken very seriously.

To name just a few, some necessary traits a hotel should find it its staff include:

Empathy

Warmth

Conscientiousness

Enthusiasm

Charisma

● Hotel regular reports for effective hotel management strategy

Reporting on performance is essential to hotel management. You need to collect and analyse accurate data regularly to see where things are working, and what you need to improve on. There are a lot of different parts of the business you'll need reports on to inform your overall strategy. Most of them can be pulled from the systems that you're using such as your property management system and channel manager etc.

Some of the most important information your hotel different department managers need to track includes:

Channel performance

Website performance

Housekeeping

ADR – Average daily rate

Occupancy

RevPAR – Revenue per available room

TrevPAR – Total revenue per available room

Channel performance is key. You need to understand a number of factors about your booking channels. For instance, which channel is delivering the most reservations? Which channel is contributing the most overall revenue? Which channel has the highest cancellation rate? Which has the largest or smallest lead time?

The point is the more information you have about your channel performance, the more tweaks you can make to optimise your distribution mix. Cutting some channels and connecting others, or temporarily pausing, can enable you to maximise revenue.

Given how important direct bookings are, website performance is equally important. Since your booking engine can be included in channel performance you'll be able to see if direct bookings are down. Investigating your website is a good idea. How much traffic are you driving via organic and paid means? What pages are being visited the most? What's the conversion rate on calls to action? How many people are abandoning a booking part of the way through?

Housekeeping is extremely significant. Do you know how long it's taking to clean a room on average? How many guests are arriving to find their room isn't ready yet? Do you have enough cleaning resources or not enough? How efficient are staff?

This is all information you need to report on each and every month to see if your business is on an upward spiral or if standards are dropping. Through your property management and revenue management systems you can track occupancy, ADR, and many other metrics.

- Hotel management software technological strategy

Technology in the hotel industry continues to advance at a rapid pace and hotel management software (HMS) remains essential for hoteliers looking to improve the running of their business. With software, hotel operators can streamline their administrative processes and improve their overall hotel management system. The key to reaping the benefits of an effective hotel management software system is to select the right one for your property. It's critical that you know exactly what this hotel management technology is, and why it is important for you to implement it at your hotel.

What is hotel management software?

Hotel management software is technology that allows hotel operators and owners to streamline their administrative tasks while also increasing their bookings in both the short- and long-term. Your hotel management system is not only important for your own day-to-day operations, but it's a vital part of the overall guest experience. From the beginning of your guests' online booking journey until the completion of their stay and their feedback once they return home, it is necessary for your hotel management technology to enhance their experience with your brand. Finding a hotel management system that offers the features you both need and want is necessary to effectively managing your hotel in a global economic climate.

The purpose of management systems for hotels

Management systems serve several purposes for both hotel operators who manage large chains as well as independent hoteliers. These include:

1. Managing bookings

Your property management system should help you efficiently and effectively manage your bookings. Neither you, nor your staff, should be tasked with manually inputting bookings and managing those across all your distribution channels. A property management system should automate the booking process for you, allowing you to escape the back office and focus more on interacting with your guests. In addition, it significantly reduces the risk of overbooking your rooms, which directly improves the guest experience at your property.

2. Direct bookings

It should allow you to actively drive direct bookings to your website. Travellers today are more apt to book online than they are to call to finalise bookings or partner with a travel agent. Direct bookings allow you to maximise the revenue that you generate per booking. You should only consider software that integrates with an online booking engine.

3. Channel management

Hotel management technology should allow you to easily implement your distribution strategy. Creating partnerships with different types of agents in the industry, such as OTAs and GDSs, is necessary to survive in a competitive, global climate. Managing hotel with software that offers a channel manager will allow you to create and implement a diverse distribution strategy that continually drives bookings.

4. Hotel website

Your hotel administration department software should help enhance your online presence. Your hotel management system is only effective if your guests can reach your brand. Choosing a program that offers a web editor or website creator will allow you to create a clean, appealing and user-friendly website that will encourage guests to book a stay at your property.

Benefits of hotel management technology

When you are selecting hotel management technology for your property, you should consider the many benefits that this system will offer you, including:

1. Reduce time spent on administrative tasks

You hotel can minimise the amount of time spent on administrative tasks. The right hotel management system will do a lot of the work for you, allowing you to focus your efforts and your energy on the big picture. The technology should also provide you with valuable data on how your employees perform their duties and how this affects employee retention, satisfaction and productivity. In today's fast-paced travel environment, it's critical that you automate as many tasks as possible. A property management system can help you tremendously with that.

2. Increase your online presence

Your hotel can increase your brand presence online. Management software that is integrated with your website builder will allow you to accept direct online bookings and develop a user-friendly website. Naturally, this will increase your relevance in the search engine results and allow more travellers to discover your property during their online booking journey.

3. Build relationships with guests

Your hotel will develop a better rapport with your target

market segment, while also identifying new markets to tap into. The types of travellers who have always loved staying at your property will appreciate the improved experience. In addition, your new technology will allow you to reach out to new markets that would not have otherwise discovered your brand.

4. Manage your distribution

Your hotel will improve your reach throughout the industry. With a property management system in place that integrates with a channel manager, you will be able to advertise across many channels whilst maintaining rate parity. From the large OTAs and GDSs to individual retail travel agents, you can provide real-time booking information to your agents that will drive bookings.

5. Manage your hotel revenue and cost expenditure control

Your hotel can implement a beneficial revenue management strategy. Using innovative pricing tools that allow you to create a flexible room pricing strategy, you can maximise the revenue that you generate per room at any given moment. Pricing your rooms right is the key to succeeding in this competitive industry, and having these tools available can help you significantly.

6. Increase room bookings

Your hotel will ultimately increase your large , middle and small size room number bookings. At the end of the day, the point of every feature within your hotel management business solution is to boost the bookings that you get at your hotel. Whether your hotel wants to increase your off-season bookings or you want to expand your offerings to new market segments, you will be successful if you select the right hotel management software for your property.

● Hotel property facility management strategy

The first aspect, is your hotel safe facility system. Managing a hotel isn't all about managing the physical property, it's also about managing intangible things like reputation. Any hotel facility issues may influence hotel customers how feel your hotel service performance, for example, when your hotel customers are living in your hotel rooms, during this living period, they feel your hotel fire system is not safe, it will influnece that they choose to reduce room booking living days because they are afraid fire occurs can cause their death. So, any hotel floor fire safe property management facilities will influence any one customer makes booking room days decision whether they can extend days or shorten days to live in your hotel.

Another aspect, is your hotel online booking facility system. It's very simple. Hospitality businesses such as hotels are at risk if they don't focus attention on their online reviews and take control of their reputation management. As more and more guests turn to one another for advice on where to stay in cities around the world, the effectiveness of traditional hotel advertising is declining – while the impact of online hotel reviews is on the rise.

Failure to monitor, manage and respond to feedback will skew your hotel management strategy to issues that are unimportant to customers, as well as provide unhappy customers with ammunition for negative feedback on travel and social media sites. It can be difficult for an individual to get through their lives without significant episodes being recorded on social media channels, let alone a hotel to exist without the blemish of social media complaints.

As the impact of online bookings and digital feedback

continues to rise, the importance of reputation management rises with it. Yet while online reputation management is a trend across the hospitality sector, it is still considered an indulgence by some independent hoteliers. Part of this rationale is driven by the confusion around how to deal with both positive and negative feedback online. So here are some standard ways hoteliers can deal with online reviews – regardless of sentiment:

The most feared of all feedback online is a negative review

However, audiences are particularly savvy in determining the value of feedback, not just because the "voice" of the author is on display, but because audiences often apply a filter to their reading of any review. Consciously or subconsciously, they consider the value of any commentary, as well as the relevance of a comment to their own experiences and preferences. So a comment on the convenience of a hotel location to an equestrian events venue will be of potential importance to horse-lovers, yet entirely irrelevant to many other potential guests. Where a rational negative comment is posted, hotels do have options on how to respond.

Acknowledge and Action

For a genuine, reasoned negative comment on customer experience, it is best for hotels to respond in a timely manner (within 72 hours of posting), acknowledging the issue and describing how it will be addressed. Ideally, a follow up post will occur after actioning the issue, and showing how the experience will not be repeated. This is by far the best possible response to negative feedback, because online audiences are far more willing to value action and positive changes in behaviour, than think poorly of the initial negative experience.

Apologise and Compensate

For a negative comment which illustrates an experience that was difficult or impossible to avoid, an appropriate response is to apologise for the poor experience and to privately offer either monetary compensation, or discounts on future bookings. While this is unlikely to totally satisfy the customer with the stated poor experience, it will indicate to other customers, the prioritisation of customer experiences at the hotel. It's important to take compensation offline where possible to avoid inviting those like to complain for free stuff.

Apologise and Thank

For negative comments that focus on pedantic details, the most appropriate response is an apology for the experience and an acknowledgement that this feedback will help shape your hotel's future guest experience strategy. This is far more useful than a response which states that the comment will be passed to a customer service team, because the customer already believes that service is the problem at the property.

How to thank hotel guests for their positive feedback

While most organisations are thrilled with the prospect of positive reviews, an abundance of rave reviews can be just as suspicious to audiences as a series of negative reviews. Therefore, positive reviews also need a response.

Be Humble

Where a positive review is excessive and perhaps gushing, it is wise for firms to thank the guest for their enthusiasm, but to also acknowledge areas where you are attempting to improve. This reinforces commitment to customer service.

Be Delighted

Where positive feedback is sincere and reasoned, the best response for hotels is to express delight and appreciation for the feedback and the desire to serve again in future. This is the easiest response to deliver, but is often the least fulfilled.

Be Appreciative

Where feedback is predominantly neutral, but some aspects are highlighted as being of particular value, it is advisable for hotel managers to express thanks for the feedback and to request further advice on how the organisation could improve in specific areas. Again, try to take this conversation offline with an email or personal phone call. This enables more considered feedback to follow the initial post.

● Reputation management strategy

Reputation management is often considered difficult or time-consuming. Yet the results of research into the importance of reputation management are unarguable: the value of reputation management is substantial and growing. Understanding how to respond to feedback is not just a competitive advantage, but potentially a means of ensuring your hotel stays in business. Your hotel can easily turn complaints around and win hotel guests back – and these basic reputation management responses are your first line of defence.

Hotel property management software

Selecting the right hotel software is critical, particularly in a world where consumers are relying more heavily on their devices with each passing day. An investment this important to your overall success as a hotel operator requires you to do some research.

These are seven questions that you should ask your hotel tech provider as soon as possible:

1. How does your hotel product maintains its relevance in the hospitality industry?

While the core of a technology system may remain the same over time, the reality is that any product geared specifically towards the hospitality industry will need to adapt to changing trends and preferences from travellers. You need to ask this question so you have an understanding of how your technology will help you grow along with the industry.

2. How often can your hotel expects upgrades for your platform?

No piece of technology is perfect, and the best hotel technology providers will make sure that regular updates and upgrades are available for their clients. It's important to have an understanding of how often these upgrades will be available, and how you will be able to successfully implement the upgrades.

3. What level of customer service will I receive from your company?

Unfortunately, far too many hotel technology providers focus on hard sales tactics without much support after the purchase is complete. You will want to verify with your provider that there will be ways to contact and work with staff after the technology has been installed at your hotel.

4. Is your hotel platform secure?

Security should be a top priority of your hotel technology provider. You will want to ask about the details regarding their security features, as it's imperative that both your data and your guests' data is secure.

5. How easily can your hotel personalise your systems?

Hotel technology providers need to offer you a versatile system that includes not only the generic features that are necessary for any hotel, but also the adaptable features that allow you to personalise the platform for your particular brand. Ultimately, your investment in technology needs to result in a system that works specifically for your hotel.

6. What reporting features are available?

When your hotel begin your search for the right hotel technology, you will likely focus first on the property management system. However, you will want to discuss additional features that also are available, with some of the most important being the reporting features. Verify that you'll be able to run detailed reports using live data, as this is the only way to ensure that you can grow your brand.

7. How can your hotel accesses the hotel technology system once implemented?

Be sure that you are investing in a system that allows you to run your hotel from anywhere. You need hotel technology that is optimised for all devices, including smartphones and tablets.

Benefits of a hotel management system

When you are selecting hotel management systems for your property, you should consider the many benefits they'll offer you, including:

1. Reduce time spent on administrative tasks

Your hotel can minimise the amount of time spent on administrative tasks. The right hotel management system will do a lot of the work for you, allowing you to focus your efforts and your energy on the big picture. The technology should also provide you with valuable data on how your employees perform their duties and how this affects employee retention, satisfaction and productivity. In today's fast-paced travel environment, it's critical that you automate as many tasks as possible. A property management system can help you tremendously with that.

2. Increase your hotel online presence

Your hotel can increase your brand presence online. Management software that is integrated with your website builder will allow you to accept direct online bookings and develop a user-friendly website. Naturally, this will increase your relevance in the search engine results and allow more travellers to discover your property during their online booking journey.

3. Build relationships with guests

Your hotel will develop a better rapport with your target market segment, while also identifying new markets to tap into. The types of travellers who have always loved staying at your property will appreciate the improved experience. In addition, your new technology will allow you to reach out to new markets that would not have otherwise discovered your brand.

4. Manage your hotel distribution

Your hotel will improve your reach throughout the industry. With a property management system in place that integrates with a channel manager, you will be able to advertise across many channels whilst maintaining rate parity. From the large OTAs and GDSs to individual retail travel agents, you can provide real-time booking information to your agents that will drive bookings.

5. Manage your hotel revenue

Your hotel can implement a beneficial revenue management strategy. Using innovative pricing tools that allow you to create a flexible room pricing strategy, you can maximise the revenue that you generate per room at any given moment. Pricing your rooms right is the key to succeeding in this competitive industry, and having these tools available can help you significantly.

6. Increase bookings

Your hotel will ultimately increase your bookings. At the end of the day, the point of every feature within your hotel management business solution is to boost the bookings that you get at your hotel.

Hotel property management system

All hotels need some variation of a property management system (PMS). However they come in many different forms and are not all created equal. There are still properties trying to manage their business in a traditional way with books and ledgers, others are using server-based systems, while many used web-based systems.

One of the most valuable things to a hotel manager is time, and money of course. The first two systems listed are a drain on both time and finances, while the latter has obviously become the optimal way to manage hotel operations. Cloud-based PMSs are a superior way to automate and accelerate all the important processes at your hotel such as taking and confirming bookings, managing reservations, generating bills and reports, check-in/out, room transfers, checking/editing availability, guest communication, the list goes in. Cloud-based technology can handle all these tasks with ease because of its ability to deeply integrate with channel managers, booking engines, and revenue management systems. Despite this, there are still concerns over the validity and cost effectiveness of cloud-based PMSs.

Here are five common property management system myths and why we think they're unfounded?

1. You think cloud-based technology is confusing or hard to use

Because it's intangible and seemingly floating in the air, some hotel managers believe using cloud technology will be hard to learn and too confusing to keep track of. The opposite is true. A PMS allows you to keep everything in one place and it can never be lost. You can access your data from any location so long as you have the Internet. The many tasks that you perform using multiple programs or books can be done from one central location with a fully integrated PMS. This also means you can collaborate better with other staff who need access to the same information.

2. You worry that sensitive data is insecure and vulnerable

While the information in your cloud PMS isn't kept under lock and key it is encrypted and backed-up. Nothing is stored 'onsite' so even if your computer breaks or your laptop is lost, your data will remain accessible to you. With data in the cloud you don't have to worry about viruses or bugs, and hacking is much less likely to succeed thanks to firewalls and authentication gateways.

3. Your current software works just as well as cloud-based technology

It's unlikely this is true and even if it is, it won't be for long. Cloud software is constantly being updated and evolved meaning users automatically get the benefits included in their monthly fee. If your current server isn't updated, it becomes slow and vulnerable, while updating it requires extra time and greater cost that has to be done too regularly.

4. You believe a web PMS is only suitable for large hotels

The reality is that smaller or independent hoteliers are often stretched thinner than anyone. With less staff and more responsibility, the time and hassle saved by using a cloud-based PMS is vital and could be the difference between getting the bookings needed for maximum occupancy or losing revenue on empty rooms.

5. You think hotel technology is too expensive

Cloud-based systems are actually very cost effective. You never require any additional hardware, backup solutions, licensing, updates, fixes. There's also no lengthy setup process and with the time you save using it, more resources can be directed towards increasing guest experience and revenue streams. Overall a cloud-based PMS will give you more control over your hotel business, with:

List of hotel property management systems may include as below:

There are literally hundreds of property management systems on the market. The most important aspect when choosing one is to ensure it's easy to use, has all the functions you need, and that it is able to integrate with your other important systems, such as your channel manager.

Some popular examples you might come across include:

Little Hotelier

Mews

Sirvoy

CloudBeds

Frontdesk Anywhere

eZee Frontdesk

Hotelogix

Maestro

OPERA

Avvio

Online booking engine

Essential if your hotel wants to capture direct bookings and reduce the commission you pay to online travel agents (OTAs). The majority of travellers will visit your hotel website even if they discover your property on an OTA.But if you're looking to capitalise on this traffic, your booking engine needs certain features beyond booking as a minimum including:

Seamless online experience for your guests via a customised, two-step booking process. Multi-language and currency capabilities to convert guests from around the globe. Mobile-friendly and Facebook-compatible to reach travellers on-the-go. Upselling capability so you can offer a more personalised stay for your guests. However your hotel booking engine can be a much more powerful tool that you can customise to suit any marketing strategy, allowing your business to maximise its revenue.

Ensure your hotel gets as much value as possible out of your booking engine by following these steps:

1. Prioritise booking engine and website integration
Seamless integration between booking engine and website will make a guests booking experience so much easier. It will be more responsive to mobile, put less pressure on you to design the look of your booking engine, and will maintain your branding throughout the entire booking process. All of this will enhance the trust your customers have in your hotel.

2. Create a strong foundation for search engine optimisation
While not directly related to your booking engine, SEO is vital. If your website isn't optimised for SEO it won't matter how amazing your booking engine is, you won't be attracting sufficient traffic to drive bookings.

3. Implement urgency messages
Urgency messages do exactly what they imply; invoke urgency in the shopper. By drawing attention to rates through urgency messages you can make your guests think they are in danger of missing out, or else getting something other customers aren't. They're a great way of speeding up the booking process and increasing conversions. Examples include 'Book now, pay later!' or 'Only two rooms left!'.

4. Use promo code banners
If you're running a promotion, you want guests to notice it. Display a prominent promo banner on your website using

your booking engine so guests can easily view and select applicable dates and benefit from the promotion.

5. Set up an early-bird rate

By selling discounted early-bird rates you can improve your short-term cash flow by collecting full prepayment from the booker. You can control when to flag an early-bird rate via your booking engine extranet.

6. Introduce last-minute rates

Setting attractive last minute rates are good for increasing your short-term occupancy or filling any remaining rooms. Offset the rate by taking a high deposit to limit the amount of cancelled bookings or no-shows. Clearly display these and use them in conjunction with urgency messages.

7. Entice guests with a stay pay deal

Maintain your occupancy by increasing the length of your guests stay. Offer them a discount for one or more of their dates, clearly indicating the price difference and encourage them to book additional nights. Make sure you have control over what night is to be discounted; first, last, cheapest etc.

8. Interest guests in package deals

Packaging up extras like entry to events, attractions, or restaurants gives guests a one-stop shopping experience that they enjoy. Offer options guests can't find on OTAs and again entice them to stay longer. If used intelligently a booking engine can be a hotel marketing and branding tool that will incentivise guests to become loyal to your hotel, further increasing your direct bookings and revenue in the future.

Hotel room management software: Channel managers

A channel manager is a tool that will allow you to sell all your rooms on all your connected booking sites at the same time. It will automatically update your availability in real-time on all sites when a booking is made, when you close a room to sale, or when you want to make bulk changes to your inventory. There's a lot more to a channel manager than simply making life easier for when updating your rates and availability. You can use it to perform many tasks when managing your hotel and its benefits are two-fold in how it can increase bookings and revenue, and enable long term business planning.

Take a look at this comprehensive list of how a channel manager can be used to benefit a hotel.

1. Increase online bookings

With telephone and walk-in bookings on the decline and online bookings on the rise, a channel manager places you in the best position to take advantage of this new traveller booking habit. Connect to more online channels, where more travellers than ever are locking in their stays.

2. Increase hotel revenue

Given a channel manager displays live rates and availability across all your channels at the same time, and updates automatically you can accept bookings faster and almost eliminate the chance of double bookings. In addition, the data you can analyse from your channel manager can ensure your rates are always optimised and you're using the most lucrative channels.

3. Reduce the risk of overbookings

Without a channel manager, you're forced to split your inventory between channels and risk double-bookings or failing to reach full occupancy. Pooled inventory and automated updates of availability and rates in real time means guests can only ever book a room that is actually available.

4. Improve brand recognition

A powerful channel manager will provide two-way unrestricted access to hundreds of booking channels where travellers who would never hear of you can now make reservations at your property. It also makes OTAs more likely to accept your listing because they can be sure your inventory will always be accurate.

5. Boost direct bookings

It may seem illogical but it's true! Many travellers will discover your property first on an OTA, but they want to learn more about you before they book. Often they will visit your website and then make the decision to book their stay. So you get a direct sale, but it was born on the OTA site – resulting in greater profit for your hotel. This is known as the billboard effect.

6. Remove manual processes

Manual data entry is time-consuming and frustrating, we all know that. If you were to use a channel manager and remove this friction, you'd realise just how much more productive you can be. Anything that has to be put on hold can now be prioritised to improve your business.

7. Create a seamless, integrated tech stack

Instead of being required to update information in multiple extranets, a channel manager can integrate with your property management system, central reservation system, or revenue management system as well as your booking engine to create a central control system for the entirety of your hotel's operations. Some channel managers, like SiteMinder, also have a unique connection to Airbnb. Although boutique hotels have already been using Airbnb for some time, there hasn't been a solution for them to manage this channel in conjunction with other partners such as online travel agents – until SiteMinder's partnership.

8. Transform into a powerful business platform

A good channel allows complete transparency of data

across all systems and channels, meaning you can use the received information to see which channels or rooms are performing the best. This means you can constantly update your business strategy. Look at reports such as channel yield and channel analysis and your reservation trends to see where things are going right – or wrong!

9. Reduce reliance on traditional booking channels

There's certainly no suggestion that you should leave behind traditional methods such as taking reservations over the phone or via walk-ins. It can be very profitable to save some of your inventory for these methods. However, using a channel manager will ensure you don't have to worry about filling your rooms in this manner. Connecting to a significant number of online booking sites will ensure your occupancy always remains steady.

10. Keep everyone on the same page

Quality channel managers are very easy to use and hotels will regularly have multiple staff members using the system. If the main user is going away or won't be available to make updates they can easily mark important dates in the system so everyone is aware if they need to change a rate or a close a room etc. For example, they may mark school holiday periods so rates can be increased during these peak times.

Hotel management apps technology

In order to enhance productivity at your hotel, you must first ensure you and your team are as organised as possible. This may be easier said than done when you have emails arriving non-stop, content to post and people to manage . Technology has evolved to solve almost any problem. There are many apps in the market to help with everyday challenges. Organised teams get more done and having everything under control also gives you a better grip on the overall success of the business.

Here are five hotel apps to help stay on top of hotel management:

1. Pocket

Have you ever come across interesting articles, videos or websites and ended up forgetting about them? Whenever you find something you want to view later, you can add it to your Pocket – an application and web service for managing reading lists. You can save content directly from your browser or from apps like Twitter, Flipboard, Pulse and Zite. Once saved to Pocket, the list of content is visible on any device (phone, tablet or computer) with access to your account – online and offline helping you share interesting articles with your hotel's team.

2. Astro

If a large part of your day-to-day duties includes sending and receiving emails, Astro will help you focus on what is most important. Astro brings along email and calendar features, powered by an Artificial Intelligence (AI) assistant, which will prioritise your emails, tell you what to follow up on, and help you clean up your inbox. Astro also adds reminders, snoozed emails, and scheduled emails to your calendar, so you can get a complete view of your day. You can also customise the emails you send with Open Tracking, Send Later, Custom Signatures, and much more.

3. Google Calendar

One of the most important parts of management is time management and having your calendar with you on the go can be crucial. Stay on track with your appointments and tasks with Google Calendar. Your events or any meeting requests received via Gmail can be automatically added to your calendar and you'll spend less time managing your schedule. Add images and maps to your appointments, and access your schedule for the day, week and month from any device at any time. You can also gain visibility of your team's work schedule and share your calendar view with them so you can make the most of your day.

4. Trello

Stay up to speed with your team projects using Trello – an easy, free, flexible, and visual way to manage and organise workflow. Trello is divided in boards, with lists representing the workflow. For example, you can have your Social Media Marketing board and inside the lists: To Do, Doing and Done. Every list has cards, representing tasks containing relevant information. For example, the New Years 7 Nights Promotion card will contain the specification of this promotion, such as due date, hotel team members that need to follow the task, checklists and more. As tasks progress along the way, the card will navigate to the next list. With Trello you have a clear and real-time view of the stage your project is at and you'll never lose track of them.

5. Evernote

If sometimes you feel the need for a second brain, meet Evernote – an app designed for note taking, organising tasks lists, and archiving. You can collect everything that matters in one place and find it when you need it, fast. Capture, organise, and share notes from any device and always keep your best ideas in sync and only a click away.

Evernote is not a simple note taking app, you can enhance your notes with links, checklists, tables, attachments, and audio recordings. Even handwritten notes are searchable. From initial brainstorm to finished project, Evernote will give you productivity bliss.

Apps the key to establishing self-service experiences

It's no secret modern-day travellers are becoming more accustomed to hyper-personalised and streamlined service from their hotels. In fact, if the hotel is going to deliver on its promise of quality, your guests expect a personalised and convenient experience.

Hotels can adapt to this growing need by prioritising data, technology, and connectivity. It's important to know what guests want, and also how to provide the appropriate services through hotel systems and applications. The tradition of limiting service and interaction to just your hotel staff and physical property is being outgrown by the ability of technology to automate and make many processes easier for guests. Where travellers once expected to be greeted by a front desk operator, they might now prefer the self-service experience that mobile check-in offers. Given the average person wastes an hour each week waiting in line, it's no surprise that self-service is catching on.

The self-service approach allows staff to be less transactional and focus on establishing genuine connections with guests. With technology in place, hotel employees will no longer be confined to stationary positions within the lobby or left to guess what guest expectations might be. For a better idea of the trends in this area and the enabling power of technology and connectivity, we spoke to four hotel applications to get their perspective.

Being able to adapt, meet challenges, and place yourself on a scale of personal growth is vital for a hotel manager. Hotel management is about overseeing every operation of the property. This requires knowledge of distribution strategy, finance, customer service, staff management, marketing, and more. Effective inventory management for hotels involves both creating and managing demand, and maximising returns. Revenue management is another huge part of managing your hotel. How do you get more money coming in and achieve business goals?

In the hospitality industry almost everything revolves around the customer, and they're the quickest party to point out any flaws. Good management eliminates as many mistakes as possible. Hotel management sometimes also requires the management of a restaurant.

Turn your hotel restaurant into a premium dining experience that focuses on the whole package including the food, lighting, music, decor, and wine lists. This way, your restaurant won't only be the bait to bring new customers in, but also an incentive for current guests to return when they revisit the area.

Similar to search engines such as Google, OTAs have their own algorithms for how your property will rank, meaning you need to pay close attention to how you build your profile on them. Fighting food waste at your hotel goes beyond feeding people and helping the environment – it also improves your property's bottom line. Reporting on performance is essential to hotel management. You need to collect and analyse accurate data regularly to see where things are working, and what you need to improve on. Hotel management software is technology that allows hotel operators and owners to streamline their administrative tasks while also increasing their bookings in both the short- and long-term.

Managing a hotel isn't all about managing the physical property, it's also about managing intangible things like reputation. There are many apps in the market to help with everyday challenges. Organised teams get more done and having everything under control also gives you a better grip on the overall success of the business.

- Keys to an effective hotel distribution strategy

How to increase your hotel's occupancy rate
Effective revenue management strategies for hotels
Essential strategies to increase your hotel room sales

Facility management, or FM, is a broad discipline that includes a variety of industries, from food to technology, manufacturing to e-commerce and beyond. But, though the core of each business may be completely different from even its closest competition, successful facility management practices are easily interchangeable from enterprise to enterprise. As a matter of fact, it is one of the only job titles that can be found in, basically, any small to large organizations, including public entities, like schools and hospitals, to private businesses, like those that manage their inventory in warehouses.But, reciprocal tendencies aside, facility management procedures and techniques must be highly-specialized for the business in which they are being used. Because the discipline covers complex specifics, including business continuity planning and even fire safety, it's key that your organization offers a holistic outlook on its facility management procedures.

- The Core Competencies of Hotel Facility Management strategy

According to the International Facilities Management Association (IFMA), facility management is an interdisciplinary practice that "considers the coordination of people, place, process, and technology." Broken down, this means that a facility manager is responsible for the success of the all facets of the facility, including organization, safety, security, and maintenance, along with the key, everyday operational practices. Facility Management Core Competencies

It may seem like an overwhelming job to put on one person or one small team – and it is an overwhelming job – but what's important to remember is the fact that facility management is just one aspect of what makes a healthy business. Simply put, all necessary departments must work with facility managers to build a business' overall success.

Safety – It's the facility management team's job to ensure the safety of all of the employees and customers occupying the property. This responsibility spans all possible environmental health and safety issues, particularly ones that concern the building and its equipment, specifically. Failure to do so can mean serious business in the form of fines, lost business, or even prosecution if it was deemed that the manager or business' negligence caused casualties or permanent environmental damage. Fire, for example, is usually right at the top of the radars of facility managers because it's a preventable tragedy that, when prepared for sufficiently, can save lives and valuable inventory. A thorough facility management team can protect its company best by guaranteeing that all parts of the facility are up-to-code, its employees are trained well, and all permits and certificates are completely valid. This function entails everything from safe and efficient lighting to flooring choices.

Security – In regards to importance, second to safety is facility security, yet another important piece of the puzzle in which the facility management team must answer to. Though larger companies or ones with particularly pricey inventory or equipment might make the wise choice to outsource its security needs in the form of a private firm, it's still the role of the facility manager to ensure that the firm performs competently. Technology advancements like biometrics and wearables are making it possible to maintain strict access control for high-security areas, but it's up to facility managers to stay on top of these developments and make smart security technology investments. In addition to general safety, it's also important that the facility management team has the technological know-how to safeguard and maintain its priciest hardware. This role is a key one as it doubly affirms that assets are protected just as closely as the safety of the community.

Maintenance and Inspections – No matter the focus of the organization, one of the most heedless things that a facility management team can do is slack off on its building maintenance duties. Every part of the building, including installed machinery such as HVAC systems, must be maintained by the facility management team. Because some facilities contain countless elements that need regular maintenance, establishing and following strict maintenance schedules helps to ensure that all moving and permanent parts of the facility stay up-to-date and working well into the future. Along with general maintenance, inspections are also something that facility management teams must always be ready for. They can prepare the business by conducting internal inspections, as needed, for the many formal regulatory inspections they might incur annually. Of course, the team must also take into account any time the facility undergoes a major change in hardware, level of inventory, or capacity – and, they must also keep their eyes on all changes in laws that could affect their current procedures.

Business Continuity Planning – Part of leading an effective facility management team means planning for "worst case scenarios." This means that each team must sit down with the powers that be to come up with a plan in case disaster strikes and the business can't afford to shut down operations. For example, let's say that a community college endures a major fire and the authorities have deemed the entire main building a total loss. The community college is currently in the middle of a semester which it can't cut short – this is a situation where prior business continuity planning is key. If this were done in the aforementioned scenario, the facility management team would have already come up with alternate locations to hold classes and operate the organization's administrative duties. In addition to the new venue, the team would have already made a solid plan for the temporary facility's security, maintenance, and hardware needs.

Daily Operational Duties – In addition to serving as the safety and security liaisons for the facility, it's also important that facility management teams are organized to handle the inherent day-to-day challenges that might arise. Depending on how the given organization is structured, this can mean anything from mending a leaky roof in the women's restroom to even fixing a jammed fax machine.

Maintenance Operations

No matter the size of the organization, it's key that the higher-ups bring on a facility manager that can hire or outsource a reliable, competent team. And, because not every company is filled with safety-minded individuals, it is the job of this manager to act as an advocate for the workers and/or customers that occupy their facility. Having this level of tenacity and attention-to-detail in the facility management spectrum is necessary – in fact, it can save a business or even a life.

Operations and Management Strategies

The current presiding global facilities management organization, the International Facility Management

Association, calls for these leaders to take a more tactical and shrewd approach when it comes to protecting the future of their business' properties. In the IFMA's Strategic Facility Planning white paper, the organization makes a call for facility managers to carry out SFP (strategic facility planning) as it "helps to avoid mistakes, delays, disappointments, and customer dissatisfaction." In addition to the aforementioned safety and maintenance-heavy responsibilities, the IFMA wants managers to begin looking beyond their normal duties so that they can better aid in the efficiency of their organizations.To do this effectively, managers must compile two things: 1) a strategic facility plan and 2) a master plan for the facility. Let's take a look at how each one can better strengthen the overall productivity of the business:

Strategic Facility Plan (SFP) – In order to compile a comprehensive SFP, the IFMA urges managers to first become acquainted with three very important things: the core values or changing values of the organization and how facilities must reflect the values, the compiling of an in-depth analysis of the facility, including location, capability, and condition, and, finally, a fundamental understanding of how the organization's goals might make for the ramping up or down in regards to facilities. If the manager can confirm each and every one of these benchmarks with the appropriate departments and find a way to support their organization's ambitions while carrying out effective day-to-day practices, then they will be acting as a truly "strategic" support system. This blend of "current" and "future" allows for all parties involved to grapple with changes as they come in the most effective manner possible.

Facility Master Plan – Any facility manager should already be constantly re-working their facility's master plan, a framework that looks at the "physical environments that incorporate the buildings," but that doesn't mean that each is as comprehensive as it could be. Let's take a look at what a holistic master plan that takes both the day-to-day tasks as well as the future space use analyses into consideration.

Here's what a facility master plan in a hotel should include:

Zoning, regulation, covenant assessments
Space standards/benchmarks descriptions
Program of space use
Workflow analyses
Engineering assessment and plan
Block, fit, or stacking plans
Concept site plan or campus plan
Architectural image concepts
Long-term maintenance plan
Construction estimates
Phasing or sequencing plan (the sequence or projects)

Once a hotel facility manager does the proper footwork to make contact with all departments that influence their facility, they will be better equipped to support their organization as it makes profitable moves in the future.

Project Management for Streamlined Facilities

Because the name of the game for facility managers is safety, maintenance, and planning, it surely comes as no surprise to you that the manager must also develop and execute a laundry list of projects to ensure that everything on and in the building is running smoothly. Facility Management Equipment Log.

Here are some examples of how project management tactics can streamline a facility's overall efficiency:

The establishment of project schedules that include both scope and budgetary needs

Advising all workers, including employees and consultants, on development and work progress

Maintaining transparent databases on each and every project to ensure that higher-ups are advised of any changes to schedule, budget, or manpower in real time

The compiling of comprehensive training schedules to ensure that all employees are properly certified for any regulatory changes that may arise

Conducting budget estimates for all proposed construction projects

Coordinating any service or maintenance upgrades for the facility's systems

Conduct meetings and get approval for necessary space alterations which might be necessary for the modernization of the space

Developing internal audit processes to ensure that all applicable regulatory standards are met, including the new ISO 41001, Facility management – Management systems – Requirements with guidance for use

Hotel Facilities Demand Organization

Best Leadership Practices for Facility Managers

Facility management is a big, often complex job that requires a strong, forward-thinking, and most of all, responsible leader who thinks about their facility's needs in as holistic of a manner as possible. In addition to possessing these qualities, the most informed managers either have years of diverse industry experience under the belt or have earned a specialized degree in the discipline. Continuing education is also common in the field, and there are a number of facilities management courses that can help facility managers stay up-to-date on current trends and best practices.

Facility Management Role

So, now that we have an idea of what an adept facility manager might look like on paper, let's delve into the most effective leadership practices they can implement to guarantee the safety and efficiency of their organization:

They are on the same page as the higher-ups in regards to the future – As mentioned throughout this guide, being a powerful facility manager means looking ahead into the future. From compiling business continuity plans in the event of a disaster to keeping an open line of communication with other departments, the manager understands that they will only be a true leader if their facility and staff are ready to roll with the changes.

They know how to plan and budget – Facility managers know the current value of every part of their facility's infrastructure – and how much it will take to upgrade. They also have an acute understanding of how their budgetary needs might ebb and flow moving forward so that they can accurately propose budgetary changes to the powers that be.

They have a feel for developing a great team – Depending on the specific needs of the organization, the facility manager might be responsible for the hiring and training of the facility workers, contractors, or even consultants. This means that the manager needs to have an innate understanding of the duties and restraints of each position and how they can best work together to make the most capable team possible. Remember, these team members are ultimately in control of the safety and security of the facility, very important jobs that can break an organization in regards to liability if something were to go awry.

They are willing to listen – It's only natural for facility managers to become frustrated with higher-ups calling for big shifts who might be physically disconnected with the facility, but that doesn't mean that they are wrong. Dynamic leaders collaborate with all departments by listening to their propositions and ideas. By doing so, they create an open, safe line of communication that, no matter the outcome, will strengthen interdepartmental relations.

Hotel Facility management is a challenging job, and it's one that grows increasingly complex as technology advancements reshape old processes into newer, streamlined approaches. The best facility managers understand exactly how to balance smart technology investments that boost efficiency while minimizing risks (e.g., fiscal and safety risks) for a positive influence on the bottom line. In short, facility management is the backbone of operations across a multitude of industries today.

In business world, the perspectives of entrepreneurial Strategies are crucial for growth. Driven by this urge, the strategic management has modeled concepts and principles towards this managerial cause. In its approach, the strategy evaluates the business operational environment and focus on the inner working of a company. In this case, it develops methodological advances and ideas that follow and target at predicting the transformation of the management practice. This paper aims to examine the strategies of management employed by the Marriott Hotels executives. For example, The Marriott Hotels choose the 'generic' strategy.The differentiation Strategy is the 'generic' approach chosen by The Marriott Hotels to market it products in the highly competitive hotel industry. Marriot International is an enterprise that has successfully employed the business-level generic strategies. The business is a global franchise or and a lodging and hotel facilities entity. These products display the Marriott facility to be the one of the top players in the accommodation sector, and the phenomenon is projected to be stabilised for a number of future years. This projection is anchored on the various competitive advantages at the disposal of the company (Marriott International Brands 34). These advantages include cost, uniqueness, and their competitiveness extent. The Marriott Global Incorporation follows a variety of strategies at the entrepreneurial level. The plans are showcased by the Marriott's vast brand portfolio that enables them to command a strong market presence in the hospitality industry. This approach is part of the strategy for the entity persuinng differentiation. The Marriot Incorporation differentiation plan is factored in developing a service and product that satisfies, in a unique way, the need of its customer. The approach is affected by the provision of several options of lodging that ranges from average to premium priced packages. The secret of value-addition offered by the uniqueness of the firm warrant it to peg a higher premium charge for hotels in the upmarket.

The way through which Marriott Hotels is implementing its strategy of differentiation

For example, Marriott Hotels is implementing its strategy of differentiation by integrating its market segmentation strategies with its every operation step. The Marriott management immediately realized, from the beginning, that one brand of the whole hotel enterprise could not offer adequate catering to every need of the guests (Harmon 2). As a result, the hotel chain utilized an extensive strategy of differentiation by creating various hotel brands. Each of the product names offered services to varied clients in the hospitality market. In this strata, products range from the low-end to high-end services. The upscale offers comprise of such products as Marriott JW Resorts, Ritz Carlton and Spas that are packaged for customers who desire luxurious and high-end accommodations (Marriott International Brands 34). Others are the Marriott Courtyard with a designed in-room space offices for the business traveler. The Fairfield Inn product offers quality service for the budget travelers. This mix of a variety of brands ensures that the Marriott International meets and fulfills any desire of every consumer regardless of her or his purchasing power. In this segmentation, the JW Marriott, Ritz Carlton, Marriott Resorts, and Hotels are promoted towards the clients desiring more experience in upscale lodging. These customers also have a strong will to pay a relatively higher cost of an added luxurious amenity. The Marriott Courtyard segment offers the business travelers an office space set-up in their units where they may be productive after business trip hours. Springhill Suites segments is a hotel offering that is moderate for a family or a single traveler with living area for unwinding before embarking on a good rest at nights (Harmon 2). The Townplace Suites and Residence Inn give accommodations an extended stay for traveler's searching for a place that is more like home. These hostels encompass living areas, full-size kitchens and sleeping quarters. In addition, the hospitality chain has a budget traveler suite with accommodations of Marriott quality. In overall, the firm has as a Marriott for all form of occasions. These products and helps the chain in its noble mission of molding loyalty to its customers. As illustrated, through this segmentation Marriott Hotels has implemented its strategy of differentiation in a unique way.

Evaluation of the Marriott Hotels' current strategy in the light of the analysis

In my opinion, the market segmentation strategy used by the hotels is a proper approach to creating a wide base of consumer. There is success for the company in this strategy, especially by segmentation its market in threefold and allocating specific price to each brand. These three categories of products. For example, the company has substantially served the high-end market in the Marriott JW Resorts, Ritz Carlton, and Spas products that are packaged for customers who desire luxurious and high-end accommodations. In addition, The Marriott Courtyard segment offers the business travelers an office space set-up in their units where they may be productive after business trip hours (Harmon 2). Springhill Suites segments is a hotel offering that is moderate for a family or a single traveler with living area for unwinding before embarking on a good rest at nights. The Townplace Suites and Residence Inn give accommodations an extended stay for traveler is searching for a home-like place. As a result, every consumer need is properly and adequately catered for without compromise in the high-quality service pursued by the Marriott Hotels management.

In my opinion, the hotel has other strategies that it may exploit. These include the Franchising and the approach Cost Leadership in its marketing mix. In addition to the market segmentation, the company should try to strengthen each brand as per its category. In this case, the firm will be able to create a strong brand identity with its consumers at all its levels of the market. As a result, it will be able to capture the mass market for its products. The increased demand will enable the firm to move high volumes of products thereby increasing its turnovers. As a result, it will be able to design a proper pricing system, as high turnovers will have high-profit levels. In addition, the company may employ the franchising strategy. In this case, it will be able to forego its traditional direct control of its hotels especially in the economies overseas. As a result, it might now concentrate its crucial business (Harmon 2). Furthermore, it will win in substantially reduce the financial risk associated with enormous businesses while allowing a more non-participatory global growth. The company may use this opportunity of franchising, as many investors are willing to collaborate with it due to its strong Marriott brand. This strategy will offset the threat of stiff competition the company is facing from its rival as Hilton and other hotels.

- Hotel cost / expense control management strategy

For hotel owners looking to grow their business, a robust revenue management strategy is of the utmost importance, helping to optimise business results. However, under the broader revenue management umbrella, there are many smaller strategies that can help to facilitate growth. In this article, you find nine revenue management strategies that those in the hotel industry can employ to achieve this ultimate objective.

What is Revenue Management?

Revenue management is a popular concept within the hotel industry, and is used to optimise a hotel or resort's financial results by maximising revenue. The accepted definition is: selling the right hotel room, to the right customer, at the right time, for the right price, via the right channel, with the best cost efficiency.Typically, it requires businesses to make effective use of performance data and analytics to predict demand, establish a dynamic pricing model and maximise the amount of revenue that the company brings in. Although revenue management is applicable to other industries, it has significance in the hospitality industry because hotels deal with a perishable inventory, fixed costs and varied levels of demand. Revenue management is considered important because it takes the guesswork out of key pricing decisions. More extended information about revenue management you can read in the article "What is revenue management?".

Revenue Management Strategies

1. Understand Your Market

In order to implement a successful revenue management strategy, it is imperative that you have a clear understanding of your market, where demand comes from and the various different local factors that might affect seasonal demand. You also need to be aware of your audience and their needs, wants and expectations.

Learn From Our Expert Partners

Moreover, you need to understand the competition that exists within the market and make strategic decisions regarding price, discounts and advertising with this competition in mind. Remember, this competition may not always be obvious, and may not always be in the same location as your hotel.

2. Segmentation and Price Optimisation

The concept of selling the right room to the right person at the right price requires you to appropriately segment your customer base. To do this, you need to identify different 'types' of customer and then look at these different segments and evaluate when they book hotel rooms or hotel facilities, how they book them and other habits. When this is carried out, it allows you to optimise prices for those different segments. One of the key advantages of this is that once prices are optimised for a particular segment, price changes can be minimised. This, in turn, can help to generate customer loyalty from those who appreciate the price consistency you offer.

3. Work Closely With Other Departments

Next, it is important to achieve close collaboration between the various different hotel departments, such as sales and marketing, in order to ensure that your revenue management strategies and their individual departmental strategies are in alignment with one another, and so that you can address challenges collectively. Identify key departmental decision-makers and bring them on board. Work with them to make adjustments to your revenue management strategies, rather than imposing your will, which might be met with resistance. Close collaboration will also help to ensure that you are always presenting consistent messages to customers and clients.

4. Forecasting Strategies

One of the most important aspects of revenue management is forecasting, which allows you to anticipate future demand and revenue, enabling necessary adjustments to be made. Within the hospitality industry, high-quality forecasting relies on accurate records being kept, including occupancy, room rates and revenue. Most forecasting strategies rely heavily on using historical data to spot trends. For example, if you notice an upturn in business in the past three Julys, it is sensible to assume the same may occur next time. However, forecasting also requires an awareness of current bookings, competitors' performance, local events and wider industry trends.

5. Embrace Search Engine Optimisation

Search engines offer one of the single biggest opportunities for those operating in the hotel industry to attract customers, which makes search engine optimisation an important part of a robust revenue management strategy. Through SEO, hotel owners can improve the visibility of their website on search engine results pages. As a consequence, you can improve the chances of attracting business from customers who are not specifically searching for your hotel, but who are searching for a hotel in your location. To achieve this, it is best to operate a solid content marketing strategy, and ensure your website's design is optimised for SEO purposes.

6. Choose the Right Pricing Strategy

There are many different pricing strategies out there, and no one strategy will guarantee success. Instead, those in the hospitality sector need to consider the best strategy for their particular hotel, based on what they have to offer, who they are trying to attract and what strategy their competitors are employing. A competitive pricing strategy, where prices are set based on other hotels prices, puts your business in direct competition and is good when your hotel has more to offer than your rivals do. Yet, in slow seasons, a discount strategy might be best, because a low-paying customer is better than an empty room. Another option is the value-added approach, where rates are higher, but additional value is provided through extras and freebies.

7. Incentives For Direct Bookings

While it is certainly important to cater for all distribution channels and meet customers where they are, rather than where you want them to be, it is also sensible to try to maximise the number of direct bookings that are made. The primary reason for this is because direct bookings do not require the commission to be paid to third parties, which means they are ideal for maximising revenue. One option is to offer exclusive incentives, such as loyalty points, or freebies, for customers who book directly through your own website.

Increase Revenue by Outsourcing Revenue Management

Revenue management is a proven concept, based on the idea of using data and analytics to optimise financial results. It also requires specific skills and knowledge, which means that it can be more effective to outsource revenue management to a third party that specialises in this area.

8. Focus on Mobile Optimisation

For those in the hotel industry, mobile has become one of the single most important revenue streams. As a result, any hotel or resort that is operating without having prioritised mobile optimisation is already operating at a distinct disadvantage compared to their competitors. Make sure your website is optimised for mobile viewing, meaning it loads quickly, the pages display properly on mobile devices and all buttons are fully functional. In addition, you need to ensure your booking process is also optimised, so that customers can book rooms from their mobile device, without needing to switch to desktop.

9. Work With a Freelance Revenue Manager

Finally, in many cases it can be beneficial to enlist the help of a freelance revenue manager, who will be able to bring knowledge, expertise and experience into your organisation. Freelancers are used to coming into hotels and getting to work quickly, and can work as and when you need them. Appointing a full-time revenue manager internally means employing them full-time, but a freelancer will only need to be paid for the work they actually do, meaning less of their time will be wasted. Moreover, because of their established expertise, you will be able to save money on costs associated with training them.
The concept of selling the right hotel room, to the right customer, at the right moment, for the right price, via the right channel is important for maximising revenue and facilitating growth. By following the nine revenue management strategies above, owners in the hospitality industry can improve their chances of achieving this.–

● Hotel service management strategy

For hotels, successful marketing depends on addressing a number of key points. These include: what a company or an industry like a hotel is going to produce; how much a hotel is going to charge; how that particular hotel is going to deliver its products or services to the guests; and how it is going to tell its customers about its products and services. Traditionally, these considerations were known as the 4Ps of the hotel industry — Product, Price, Place, and Promotion. As marketing became a more sophisticated discipline in the hospitality industry, a fifth 'P' was added and implemented— People. And recently, two further 'P's were added, mainly for service industries (like the hospitality industry)— Process and Physical evidence. These considerations are now known as the 7 Ps of service marketing in the hotel industry and sometimes referred to as the marketing mix of the hospitality industry!

In the realm of hotels, marketing is a technique of guiding the customers to choose your goods and service rather than electing the products of your rivals. If a hotel is not accounting for this aspect to make their brand more relevant, they are hampering their profit level, sales, and occupancy. The key for all hotels is to search the correct channel of marketing (which may be Display Advertising, Email Marketing, Pay-Per-Click Advertising (PPC) or Online Public Relations) and disclosing the accurate message in order to influence the targeted guests.

How to manage luxury hotel

The hotel industry has welcomed an unprecedented level of luxury. The rising demand for this extravagance is the increasing guest pursuit of meaningful, personalized experiences that are at the same time unique, exclusive and memorable. At luxury hotels, we work with a number of hotels that offer such services. From this first-hand experience, we have seen that luxury hotel guests don't want to be seen as capricious and wasteful. They value their privacy, yet seek out luxury stays for the unique surprises and thrills that hotel management can offer.However, it may have different kinds of service peformance strategies for luxury and not luxury hotel service perfomance, it may differ as below:

Outstanding Luxury Hotel Services hotel positioning strategy

1. Paparazzi Police

Keeping their vacation private is the minimum that your guests can ask of your luxury hotel, right? But, if for instance you have celebrity guests whose daily life involves being followed by paparazzi, maintaining such privacy presents challenges.To solve this paparazzi problem, for example the Las Ventanas hotel in Los Cabos, Mexico came up with an innovative solution to ensure their guests' privacy and an enjoyable stay. This hotel's staff are equipped with reflective screens, which protect their guests from prying photographers. These "Paparazzi Police" use their screens to shine light at the photographers, which ruins their photos.

2. Personalized Firework Display

We focus on Las Ventanas again, as the luxury hotel offers a spectacular personalized, private fireworks show. Costing around $1,700 per minute, guests can easily personalize it to their liking. It is another service that helps create a truly unique, unforgettable experience in a part of the world that is known for its mesmerizing natural beauty.

3. Hot Air Balloon Ride

Breathtaking experiences are a favorite of luxury hotel guests prepared to pay extra for the privilege. One such experience is a ride in a hot air balloon. And one such hotel that offers this service is the Kale Konak Hotel, located atop Cappadocia in Turkey. Leveraging its position amid a location of natural splendor, this hotel helps its guests by organizing a hot air balloon ride, which promises a stunning experience of a lifetime.

How can your hotel take advantage of its surroundings to offer thrilling adventures and experiences?

4. Sunscreen-Spraying Booths

Hotel guests don't want to worry about anything when they enjoy the beach or the resort pool at remote and exclusive locations. And if there's one thing that can ruin a vacation, it's sunburn. Proactive hotels take it upon themselves to help guests prevent burning up by including sunscreen-spraying booths as a standard luxury hotel service. In particular, many Caribbean hotels offer this service, loved by solo travelers, couples and families alike. After all, even if a guest carelessly forgets to apply sunscreen and suffers the consequences, they are much more likely to associate your hotel with the negative experience. By offering sunscreen-spraying booths, you cancel out this possibility and create a value-added service for your guests, so they can enjoy their vacation in full.

5. Sunscreen-Spraying Booth

For hotels that are located with expansive countryside hills nearby, paragliding is a luxury service that ticks all the boxes. It can be relatively inexpensive to run, offers a riveting add-on experience, and will hep move you head and shoulders above your competition. A novel twist is to offer a paragliding route from atop a hill to the hotel entrance at the bottom. With the help of a professional paragliding expert, the most demanding and fearless of guests can enjoy an extreme sport and make a rock-star entrance at your hotel.

6. Secret, Invite-Only Room

It is an increasing trend to offer a secret or hidden service. But the catch is that it can't be bought by money. Certain luxury desires can only be attained with the right contact, recommendation, knowledge or invite. Think of the appeal of speakeasy bars, or exclusive, secret societies. Take advantage of this winning trend by creating a secret, invite-only room in your hotel. Make it exceptionally beautiful or intriguing, or offer services that are unobtainable to "regular" guests. Choose a secluded or forbidden area of your hotel for its location. And of course, this secret room cannot be advertised on your official channels, such as your website.

7. In-Suite Shopping

Luxury is never having to pack a suitcase, no matter where you go or for how long. Take inspiration from London's Hotel Café Royal, which offers its guests a personalized, curated styling service for all occasions during their stay. Guests check in without luggage and find a selection of clothes handpicked by a personal stylist to choose from in their suite upon arrival. By offering your guests this luxury option, you make them feel like pop stars. And not only is it extremely convenient, everyone loves discovering a new outfit to wear and feeling like a VIP.

8. Complimentary Luxury Car Drives

Some of the very best 5-star luxury hotels offer their guests luxury cars during their stay too, for free. Hotels like The Peninsula Beverly Hills in California provide their guests with Rolls-Royce and Infiniti cars, having developed a strong relationship with the high-end car manufacturers. If you have the budget to ramp up your luxury hotel with this complimentary service, it will help serve as a magnet for guests eager for exclusive experiential stays. And if not, there are other options. For instance, you can approach high-end car leasing companies to enquire about reaching an agreement. And it doesn't have to be luxury cars. You could also tap into the growing importance of sustainability to guests by offering premium eco-friendly cars.

9. No-Internet Digital Detox Zone

C-suite executives and stressed millionaires with companies and scores of people dependent on their decisions and attention find it difficult if not impossible to disconnect. With so much responsibility on their shoulders, they are often available around the clock, seven days a week. Even if they do get an opportunity to get some much needed time off, they are often interrupted by a colleague who needs their input on the latest emergency or major decision at their company. Cue the growing prevalence of no-internet resorts. No WiFi, no mobile internet signal and no onsite computers to access the web. Completely and utterly offline.

This digital detox is increasingly sought after by hyper-connected individuals who want to get away from it all, even if only for a few days, offering them total peace and quiet, without the fear of their phone blowing up with calls, messages and emails. For typically busy company executives and such individuals in an ultra-connected world, this kind of opportunity to unwind and relax "off the grid" is an increasingly exclusive luxury.

On conclusion, more and more hotels are trying to make their guests' stay as special as possible so in the near future, many of these unconventional services will be offered by more luxurious hotels all over the world. This being said, a great hotel manager goes beyond what customers say they want, helping them to realize their wildest dreams by combining fun, joyful experiences with exclusive, unique services that make them feel important.

For hotels, successful marketing depends on addressing a number of key points. These include: what a company or an industry like a hotel is going to produce; how much a hotel is going to charge; how that particular hotel is going to deliver its products or services to the guests; and how it is going to tell its customers about its products and services. Traditionally, these considerations were known as the 4Ps of the hotel industry — Product, Price, Place, and Promotion. As marketing became a more sophisticated discipline in the hospitality industry, a fifth 'P' was added and implemented— People. And recently, two further 'P's were added, mainly for service industries (like the hospitality industry)— Process and Physical evidence. These considerations are now known as the 7 Ps of service marketing in the hotel industry and sometimes referred to as the marketing mix of the hospitality industry!

Hence, in the realm of hotels, marketing is a technique of guiding the customers to choose your goods and service rather than electing the products of your rivals. If a hotel is not accounting for this aspect to make their brand more relevant, they are hampering their profit level, sales, and occupancy. The key for all hotels is to search the correct channel of marketing (which may be Display Advertising, Email Marketing, Pay-Per-Click Advertising (PPC) or Online Public Relations) and disclosing the accurate message in order to influence the targeted guests.

Before providing an excellent service is experienced, it first has to be delivered. It, therefore, means that the process of choosing to use a service might be perceived as risky since one is buying something that is intangible. To reduce this uncertainty, physical evidence such as case studies should be used. This can be done by keeping the facilities clean, well decorated and tidy. The physical evidence that is demonstrated by an organization should be able to confirm the assertions of the customers. Although it might not be possible for the customers to experience the service before they have purchased, the customers can talk to other customers with experience!

GUEST ENGAGEMENT GUEST EXPERIENCE HOTEL INDUSTRY HOTEL MARKETING HOTEL REVENUE MANAGEMENT MARKETING

Hotel-sales-strategies-direct-bookings

Your worst nightmare as a hotelier is walking down the halls of your hotel and realising that rooms are empty. There's a sad stillness that not only marks the sign of a quiet moment, but also the sign of a failing business strategy. In order to avoid this situation at any point during the year – even during the slow travel season – you need to implement sales strategies that will improve business and continually bring in more guests. The first, and most obvious reason, to focus on increasing hotel room sales is because this will drive revenue. With additional revenue on-hand, you are able to provide guests with the service they expect, as well as move the hotel forward into the future. Before you can dabble in additional packages, add-on excursions and luxury upgrades, you must be able to sell rooms. Another reason to prioritise hotel room sales techniques is to provide guests with the atmosphere that they expect. A vacant or nearly empty hotel is not a good look to people who are staying there. You want to be able to sell as many rooms as possible so that you can provide your guests with a lively, charismatic environment.

- Essential hotel room sales strategies

Every hotelier needs to implement sales strategies that work best for their own target market as well as for their local destination. Ultimately, it is up to the hotel operator or manager to create a customised sales strategy that will drive the most room sales at their own individual property, but these are some of the top hotel room sales strategies to consider:

1. Hotel group sales strategy

This strategy may require an overhaul of your normal marketing and sales approach. The idea is to sell rooms and meeting spaces to corporate groups; it's important you can offer a deal for both. Landing these types of sales requires innovation but it can be very beneficial for repeat business if you do. The most cost effective way to secure group bookings is by connecting directly to planners. You can list your property on venue marketplaces where planners can view floorplans, photos, and unique differentiators. It's also important to segment your target audience so you can make compelling offers to the right kind of groups for your property.

2. Hotel direct sales strategy

With this sales strategy, the priority is to earn direct bookings online from as many guests as possible. Direct bookings are the most beneficial booking for hotel operators because these bookings generate the most revenue. There are no agents or other distribution partners that must be paid a commission when a guest books directly online. In order to implement a direct booking strategy, hotel managers should invest in an online booking system that syncs with their existing website and property management system. Hotel operators should also prioritise their social media strategy when focusing on increasing direct bookings.

3. Destination marketing sales strategy
This type of sales strategy requires a hotel operator to work with other tourism business professionals in their destination to promote the region as a whole. Through a destination marketing campaign, local businesses team up to target the most powerful inbound tourism markets and drive more traffic to the general area.
4. Cross-promotional sales strategy
With this sales strategy, hotel managers need to identify and evaluate various large events that will be taking place in the local region throughout the calendar year. Then, the hotel operator needs to come up with a promotion that can coincide with the event, ultimately allowing them to earn an influx of bookings that they may not otherwise have had. Opportunities that are ideal for a cross-promotional sales strategy include an upcoming industry conference, a concert or a major sporting event.
5. Guest rewards sales strategy
Many travellers today, particularly the powerful millennial generation, value the opportunity to earn rewards with the companies that they do business with. Hotels, in particular, have great success with rewards programs. In a guest rewards sales strategy, the manager or operator should develop a system that rewards guests for staying frequently, for purchasing upgrades, and for referring friends and family members. A rewards sales strategy often generates repeat bookings, which are particularly lucrative for hotel operators.
6. Revenue management sales strategy
This type of sales strategy aims to maximise the number of rooms booked at any point in the year, regardless of the typical travel traffic at that particular point in time. Typically, a revenue management plan requires hotel

operators to drop room rates during the low season in order to encourage bookings, while raising rates during high traffic times. During these moments, guests are going to be willing to pay higher rates to get a room, so it's worthwhile raising rates to generate more revenue per available room.

Other room selling techniques in hotels

Large, overarching, strategies are vital to drive a consistent level of business at your hotel but there are other smaller tactics you can use to sell your rooms or generate more revenue from each guest:

Upselling – Upselling is the process of selling a more expensive version of the service or product your customer is buying. The methods you use to upsell need to be handled with a degree of delicacy. The timing, tone, and regularity with which you upsell is the key to the success of your efforts. You don't want to seem pushy so treat it as an exercise in awareness rather than a sales pitch. Make sure guests know what options are available to them but let them initiate any further interest.

Re-marketing – Re-marketing allows you to reach out to potential guests who have visited your site without finalising their booking. Many travellers will visit a variety of different websites to explore their options during the research phase of their online booking journey. With re-marketing strategies, you can access these customers again at different points during their online booking experience and remind them to visit your site again to book with you.

Incentives or cross-selling – Cross-selling is the process of selling an additional, supplementary product or service to complement the product or service your customer is buying. Offering incentives in the form of additional products or services may just be the thing that gets your guest to confirm a booking. Think added-value items like a free massage, or a local tour.

Build local partnerships – Unless your hotel is located in a remote or isolated destination, there should be plenty of other businesses and attractions you can form a mutually beneficial partnership with. Co-promoting with restaurants, specialty shops like ski hire, adventure companies, theme parks, or museums can help lead to easy and effective marketing. And these kind of partnerships can work no matter how the guest is planning their trip – be it to book accommodation first, or create their itinerary before looking for a hotel.

Make booking easy on your website – The importance of a good website experience for travellers can't be overstated. Nothing will drain their excitement quicker than a slow, confusing, or convoluted website. Make sure yours is clean, intuitive, mobile-friendly, and has clear action buttons such as 'book now' for potential guests to click. When direct bookings are so valuable, your website has to be a priority.

● Hotel promotion strategy

Promotions are great because you can be very flexible and targeted with what you offer, and often they'll grab the attention of travellers searching online. This is where it can actually be useful to steer into what guests might expect, such as promotions around seasons, themes, events, direct, bookings, or partnerships.

1. Seasonal promotions

Most destinations experience a low season, where tourism is not as active as other parts of the year. However, with the right deals your hotel doesn't have to suffer through empty rooms and hallways. Try to incorporate discounts with eye-catching promotions like 'Summer Getaways' and 'Winter Retreats' and remind travellers how beautiful your destination is and how much they can see when there are less crowds.

2. Themed promotions

These will be attention-grabbing and very relevant for travellers looking into booking a stay in the area. For example you might offer promotions around honeymoons or anniversaries if you're in a romantic locale, adventure deals if you're out of the major cities, or ultimate relaxation experiences if you're a coastal hotel. Appealing to different lifestyles or family setups is always a good idea.

3. Event-based promotions

It makes a lot of sense to capitalise on events and include them in your promotions. People will already be researching these events so if your hotel has a deal on in conjunction with them, awareness of your hotel should increase along with site traffic. These events might include music or art festivals, Easter or Christmas events, circuses, travelling markets, sporting events etc. With a booking you might offer discounted tickets, adapt the hotel experience to match the events, create special rates.

4. Direct booking promotions

Placing exclusive promotions within your booking engine on your website will give travellers an incentive to book direct instead of via an OTA. It will also help establish your hotel website as your most important distribution channel and help increase profit by eliminating OTA commission fees. The incentive might be a discount, or it might also be an added extra such as a bottle of wine, restaurant voucher, or amenity gift cards.

5. Partnership promotions

Combining with other businesses will reduce the cost of promotion and marketing, and give you wider coverage as long as your partner holds up their end of the bargain. It may also give you access to a new market and create ongoing business. Common partnerships include those with theme parks, restaurants, cinemas, museums, sporting arenas, adventure and tour guides. It's one thing to create your promotions, but remember you need people to see them. Always advertise on your social media channels and ensure your search engine optimisation is strong

6. Mobile-only promotions

Year on year, nearly every statistic points to an upsurge of mobile usage on hotel, travel, and booking websites, with projected numbers even more prominent. As quick as online booking overtook more traditional and outdated methods, mobile is starting to usurp desktop. Implementing smart and effective mobile strategies will boost customer experience and keep your hotel competitive within an industry that never stops innovating.

● Hotel packages strategy

Use other businesses to enrich your packages – Combining your services with that of another tourist attraction in the area is a surefire way to add value to your packages. It also gives you a lot of flexibility on what you can offer guests. Tickets to zoos, tours, theme parks, museums are always popular as are restaurant vouchers. Even concerts or one-off events can be leveraged as short-term packages. This way you can cater for many different guests, those interested in adventure and those more excited by shopping or fine dining.

Promote one-stop shopping – Savvy travellers will look at your packages and wonder exactly what kind of deal they're getting. Unless you and your business partner agree to offer discounted prices it's likely the combined price of a room and a tour package will be similar to the components purchased separately. This is why you need to advertise the convenience and quality of what you're offering, rather than spruiking the cost.

Be creative with your choices – Guests might become rather bored if they see yet another 'romance' package. Try incorporating more interesting content into your packages and their names. For instance a 'bucket list' package might include a selection of passes or discounts to the absolute must-sees of the local area. This will be an attractive option for guests because it's likely they already interested in visiting those landmarks. For business travellers, always focus on convenience such as a package delivering breakfast to their room, free dry cleaning, and transport services.

Use your own property to add value – While most packages include a room and some type of external activity, you can make your packages even more enticing by adding your own service to the mix such as spa-treatments or a bar tab. Guests will want to experience your amenities and they'll be more likely to pay to do so if it's included in a package.

Cater for speciality markets – Never ignore families. Often it's the children you're appealing to most because parents will be looking for activities that will occupy the kids. The same principle applies if you're a pet-friendly hotel. You must also consider guests with disabilities and people with specific occupations that you can give personalised packages to. Don't forget to promote any new packages you create, be they long-term or one-off. Use Facebook, Twitter, Instagram, and your email sends to drum up business. Send any information along to your local tourism office so they can do the same. Another thing to consider is what you want to achieve with your packages. Sometimes they can create a lot of brand awareness, even if they don't attract much business directly.

direct-sales-hotel

To the average traveller you and your competitors will often appear very similar. That's why you need to present an offer that tips the balance and convinces an undecided traveller yours is the best hotel for them. Package deals and extras are an easy, but extremely effective way of doing this, providing you take the right approach.

Your hotel distribution strategy and how it impacts sales Implementing a successful sales strategy requires you to have an effective distribution strategy. Hotel operators must network with industry professionals as well as agents to sell their rooms to the maximum number of people in a variety of target market segments. Common agents that are included in any distribution strategy include retail travel agents, visitor information centres, local businesses, online travel agents, and destination marketing organisations. Hotel operators and managers must recognise that their distribution network is a fluid, living entity, and they should constantly be looking for new and innovative ways to reach out to new agents and distributors.

In addition to expanding and developing a diverse distribution network, hotel operators must be able to effectively distribute their rooms to all of their agents in real-time. The only way to do this is to partner with a channel manager that connects to your property management system. With a channel manager, hotel operators can provide their live availability to every distribution agent that they have, regardless of their location or time zone. This allows them to sell as many rooms as possible — including securing those valuable last-minute bookings. It also significantly reduces the risk of overbooking rooms at the property, particularly during high-volume times. A channel manager is necessary to implement any sales strategy that a manager wishes to employ at their individual property.

Hotel sales tools

Your hotel sales tools include anything that enable you to bring a guest into your hotel. This might mean your social media accounts, your email marketing campaigns, the phone on your front desk, guest feedback, or back-end hotel technology solutions.Though when you think of tools as objects or functional pieces of software you might consider these to help inform your sales strategy:

Social networks

Analytics tools such as Google

Survey tools

Online travel agents

Property management tools

Booking engines

Channel managers

Website builders

Identifying and using the right tools will depend on your property and the guests you want to attract but for the most part all properties need the same tools. The difference comes in how you use them. Data is extremely important so using tools that can give you detailed reporting functions is a great step to take. With enough data at your disposal, you can make informed decisions about how you sell, gaining an edge over any competitors who are following a 'cookie-cutter' approach. Obviously you need to be smart about you use the budget at your hotel and look at tools which will make life easier while helping deliver more revenue to the business.

Hotel sales software

When you think of sales software in a hotel context, it's better to think distribution software. Three key pieces of technology that could help you are a channel manager, online booking engine, and website builder. While they may not be strictly thought of as sales software, they are the key to driving sales and revenue in the hotel industry.

Channel manager

This is one of your greatest allies when distributing your rooms because it's a tool that manages all the different online travel agents (OTAs) you sell your rooms through, such as Booking.com, Expedia or Airbnb. The main operating principle is called "pooled inventory" which means updates to rates and availability are made automatically across all connected channels whenever and wherever a booking is made. Enabling a more effective way to promote your rooms will naturally create an increase in sales. Read our guide on channel managers to learn more.

Booking engine

Also a reservation system, this will secure online bookings from direct channels such as your own website and social media pages like Facebook. An online booking engine has become essential, especially with the rise of social media. Creating a friction-less experience for guests when they book direct will boost your conversion and improve your sales results. Read our guide on booking engines to learn more.

Website builder

This takes away the need for you to hire a web designer. Instead you can use this software to create a beautiful, search engine optimised, guest converting website in minutes. You simply have to provide your content and choose from a number of available templates. Your website is a major selling point for travellers – winning them over with an amazing first impression is imperative. With the right technology in place, you will be able to easily and effectively implement your hotel room sales strategies. To learn more about these hotel sales tools and to find out if they are the right choice for your hotel property, check out how they work in a video demo.

What to expect from these hotel room sales strategies ? When you sell hotel rooms, you do more than just get another guest in the door of your property. You are able to improve your hotel business in its entirety. Here are a few of the benefits that you will realise when you employ hotel room sales strategies that are designed to increase hotel room sales:

You will generate more revenue consistently throughout the entire year. An effective hotel sales strategy allows you to earn as much revenue as possible, regardless of the seasonal ebbs and flows of the tourism industry. You will be able to make improvements to your property. As you begin to earn more revenue from your bookings, you can make improvements that will generate buzz about your brand and continue to sell more rooms. Finally, you will be able to move beyond standard sales strategies and begin creating packages that increase the revenue you generate per guest. Once your sales steadily increase, you can begin to expand your offerings. Romance packages, adventure packages and luxury upgrades allow you to sell more rooms while also boosting the revenue you earn per booking.

- Hotel revenue management technology

What is revenue management for the hospitality industry? Revenue management refers to the strategic distribution and pricing tactics you use to sell your property's perishable inventory to the right guests at the right time, to boost revenue growth. Other products such as your amenities and food and beverage offerings will also come into the picture. Revenue management revolves around measurement of what customers from different segments are willing to pay, and this can only be done by measuring and monitoring the supply and demand of your hotel rooms.

Every traveller has a maximum value they can offer your hotel; revenue management is about capturing as much of this value as you possibly can. Preferably you'll do this by convincing the guest to book direct, purchase extensions, up-sells or extras, and become a return visitor. The best strategies are based on the understanding that hotel pricing is fluid, and can change from one day to the next. This is why you should never be afraid to increase your rates. Customers actually expect increases over time – most businesses where consumers spend money are varying their prices based on demand and shifts in costs.

Effective hotel revenue management strategies can also help hoteliers:

Better manage resources

Protect against rostering too many staff during slow periods

Ensure adequate numbers of staff are working during the busiest times

With all this in mind, revenue management can drive the entire business plan when implemented effectively. Your hotel distribution strategy is also a vital part of your revenue management plan. Make sure you are on the internet distribution channels that promote your destination online. They have strong marketing power and can put your hotel in front of many customers you can't contact directly.

How to increase hotel revenue ? Many strategies come into play when driving more revenue to your hotel, and many of them don't involve raising prices or playing with your rates much at all. Not least of these is satisfying your customer. If the product you offer is universally recognised as quality, you have the grounding to charge a higher price. If guests feel like they are getting maximum value for their money, it's very likely they'll be willing to spend more. Getting more out each individual guest who stays with you is a great way to increase the overall revenue of your hotel. For instance, guaranteed revenue from a guest you convince to stay an extra night by discounting the additional night might be worth your while, especially in low season.

A list of general tactics you can use to improve your hotel's revenue stream:

Be bookable online

These days travellers enjoy the flexibility, convenience, and value of booking online. By connecting to online travel agents/more online travel agents you'll easily see an uplift.

Build a revenue culture

Who's on your revenue team? Everyone! Anticipatory service + proactive revenue-minded employee = emotionally connected customer with engaged loyalty and higher revenue returns.

Sell other hotel products

Revenue opportunities extend far beyond simply selling your rooms. Think about the amenities you have on site and what your are charging for them, and go even further by offering hotel guests the chance to purchase items like soap, utensils, towels etc – especially if your hotel has a unique sense of style.

Leverage events and attractions

Local events and attractions are a great opportunity to put together packages for guests or offer additional services such as transport. The benefits are two-fold – guests will enjoy their stay more and your hotel will generate more income.

As you move away from tactics and towards fully fledged

strategies around your revenue and room sales, you need to start understanding your key performance indicators (KPIs). Once you know what you should be looking at you can start analysing the data and developing ways to manipulate them in your favour.

As an introduction, these are the metrics you can explore:

Occupancy rate
ADR (Average daily rate)
RevPAR (Revenue per available room)
TrevPAR (RevPAR + ancillaries)
GOPPAR (Gross operating profit per available room)
RevPASH (Revenue per available seat hour) – useful if you have a hotel restaurant

The principle that you should always keep in mind is to assess market conditions in real-time and adapt accordingly.

Revenue management strategies

You need a revenue management strategy to remain sustainable – that's the short story. Ideally, you'll even be able to turn a tidy profit each year. The best hotel revenue management strategies recognise that hotel pricing is fluid, and can change from one day to the next. It's critical that any hotelier creates a revenue management strategy that is adaptable to the current conditions. Often it's more important to focus on your own business and be confident than to worry too much about competitors, at least at first.

Every hospitality business strategy has to have the customer at its heart. How do travellers behave in the current landscape? How do they book and travel? How do they experience and explore? What do they require? What are their expectations? It's vital you have an idea of these factors if you want to squeeze the most value out of each guest that enters your door. The better you know the guest the more guest loyalty you can generate, which is extremely important for recurring revenue. If you know you have a certain amount of guests returning each year, that's more rooms you don't have to worry about and you can focus more on upselling and cross-selling.

Hotel pricing strategies

There's no pricing strategy that is perfect for any hotel. Each property must consider the pricing strategy, or strategies, that work best for its particular brand. A revenue manager will spend a lot of time analysing data and other influencing factors to ensure the business is operating with the best possible chance to maximise income.

There are a number of questions that should surround your pricing strategies:

What do your guests want?

Which strategy will complement the business mix?

How will different strategies affect connected channels and distribution partners?

How does your strategy integrate with your channels?

Who are the experts that can help determine the right strategy?

With all that in mind, the first priority of pricing should be forecasting. This way you can predict demand so you can get travellers to book early. Then you can raise rates later as availability drops and demand increases. (This is an ideal pricing structure known as the "ascending model" whereby pricing increases closer to an arrival day.) We'll talk more about forecasting and analysis later.

What is dynamic pricing?

Dynamic pricing involves changing room rates daily or even within the day based on real-time market data. Taking supply and demand into account, prices should fluctuate regularly if you want to maximise revenue. This pricing option is well suited in today's market and is one many hoteliers opt to use.

Dynamic pricing examples

Put simply, there will be days where supply and demand will be very different depending on the time of day. In the morning you may have lower rates because your occupancy is low, as is demand. However by that evening supply may have reduced and demand grown. Many factors can drive this, such as competitors putting up their no vacancy signs or setting rates slightly too high, or travellers arriving late for events the next day and so on. You can raise your rates to take advantage of the shifting market and earn more revenue than if you'd kept your rates static.

What is open pricing?

Open pricing defines the flexibility hotels around the globe have to set their prices at different levels depending on the various target markets and distribution channels they deal with.

This luxury of choice allows hotels to forecast more accurately. For example, a high-end hotel may usually attract guests who no budget constraints but in the off-season bookings will drops and the hotel can drop rates to attract travellers who normally would not be able to afford the stay. While the average daily rate of the hotel will be lower, occupancy will remain steady and revenue will continue to turnover.

Other hotel pricing strategies

There are numerous pricing strategies you can use at your hotel as part of your broader revenue management strategy, many of them in conjunction. Here's a list of the most common pricing strategies your hotel might find useful:

1. Value-added pricing

You can set your room rates higher than the local competition while also offering more extras in the basic package. This gives the illusion that the hotel offers a premium experience that focuses on value rather than just low rates.

2. Discount pricing

Used in slow seasons to boost occupancy by dropping base rates. Revenue can be made up through other services in the hotel.

3. Price per segment

Offering the same product at different prices to different types of customers. E.g 'family rate'

Length of stay

When demand outweighs supply, it can help to implement a rule where guests are 'obligated' to stay a minimum number of days. In such cases, lower rates may not be necessary.

4. Positional pricing

Basing your rates off brand strength and reputation.

5. Penetration pricing

Positioning yourself as the cheapest in the market. Be mindful of how travellers will perceive your hotel – you need to retain the opportunity to sell at higher rates.

6. Skimming

Positioning your hotel among the most expensive. Price leaders often achieve among the highest profitability, however the consumers need to clearly understand the reasons that they would pay more for staying at your hotel.

What does hotel market segmentation mean?

Segmenting is a key aspect of revenue management. It allows you to differentiate between the travellers who are coming to your hotel and devise uniques strategies for all of them. For example, the approach you take with young adventurers will be very different to a business professional. However segmentation is more complex than simply business vs leisure, and you can use it to discover trends within your hotel business.

One of the best ways to identify and filter segments is by their reason for travel. Think family holiday, wedding, tourist event, adventure, relaxation, business, etc. However, more and more hotels are adopting a different strategy and defining market segment by how a reservation was made, e.g. Expedia as a market segment. This is known as "blended segmentation" – combining the reason for stay and method of booking. Hotel chains have adopted different applications of this traditional definition of a market segment and channels. Some hotel chains and groups identify a channel as an OTA, and then identify the likes of Booking.com's reward program and Expedia's Egencia (for corporate travel) as sub-channels.

Further segmentation factors that you should take into account include:

Length of stay
Days of the week of stays
Lead time (how long before arrival do they book)
Cancellations
No show ratio

Once you have a good grip on market segments you can start to decide which groups your business wants to focus on more, and which to close out at different times of the year. By drilling down further you might realise certain segments have higher cancellation rates and you could want to resist marketing to them. Each segment will have a unique opportunity for you to gain extra business or revenue.

Here's a quick snapshot of the possibilities:

Loyalty or rewards members – Offer discounts
Mobile booking – Use mobile exclusive promotions
Direct bookings – Make offers that only exist on your website
Walk-ins – Entice extra spending with your amenities
Corporate – A chance to negotiate rates with large companies
Online travel agents – Advertise special event packages
Groups – Combine with tour operators and attractions

Every piece of analysis you do helps you build the optimal business mix for your hotel, so it's important to look at all your options. If selling is a problem, there's always a new way to sell or new market to target. If spending is the problem, there's always a way to entice customers to open their wallets again.

Hotel price forecasting

Forecasting is not only important for rate setting, but also for budgeting purposes. Accurate and effective forecasting requires a strong foundation in historical data. By budgeting and forecasting in advance you'll have plenty of time and opportunity to make strategy adjustments. If you know one point in the year is particularly valuable to your hotel, write your forecast immediately for that period a year in advance. For example, try writing your December 2021 forecast on January 1st 2020.

Key components of an effective forecast include:

Occupancy
Revenue
Room rates
Turnaways/Regrets/Denials – tracking of reservations that are turned away or not booked, and is a critical measurement of demand. Ideally your turnaways are

captured and measured on your online as well as direct/ telephone requests.

Spend per room

Reservations

Market trends

Hotel budgeting and demand forecasting

It's a good idea to create demand calendar prior to setting your budgeting plan so you know exactly what you're dealing with. Most hotels forecast every day for next 30 days and every week for next 90 days. A lot of hoteliers do this in a spreadsheet after extracting data from their PMS, but this is where you need really cool tech – and a really easy system – that can do it all in one place.

Take into account factors from last year and also the upcoming year. Mark the following as things to track:

RevPAR last year

Groups or events last year

Demand level indicator last year (High, Medium, Low, Distressed)

Public/bank holidays

School holidays

Indications of increased demand

This will allow you to make informed pricing strategies based on solid data sets.

Before you reach your ideal budget you have to take into account influences such as sales resources, online marketing and distribution, refurbishment needs, and developments your competitor set is making. Your budget should be developed on the basis of this question: at which rate and how many rooms can you sell for every future day? For example, how do you anticipate the business demand and the leisure demand per country? At which rate can you sell on the upcoming months? How will your main corporate accounts behave?

Two distinct demand measurements are constrained demand and unconstrained demand.

1. Constrained demand

Maximum demand for amount of rooms (the maximum number of bookings you could get based on the number of rooms) limited by the physical inventory.

2. Unconstrained demand

Maximum bookings you could get with unlimited rooms based on demand and not limited by the actual physical inventory.

You should identify when unconstrained demand is above the capacity of the hotel. This is an important part of your hotel revenue management strategy. The unconstrained demand will help you calculate your Last Room Value for certain dates, and possible length of stay restrictions that may apply.

Hotel benchmarking

Hotels will commonly benchmark against their competition to evaluate performance. It's not the definitive way to track performance, nor should it be treated as an authority, but it does enable you to see where you stand and how travellers might react.

You'll be required to benchmark on criteria such as:

Prices

Product (luxury, mid-range, economy?)

Level of service

Location

Distribution channel

Remember a competitor is only a competitor if they're targeting the same markets as you, and even then you might not be competing for the same segments at the same time. However, if you can anticipate their strategies, making your own adjustments will become much easier. In the context of the competitor set, results can often look very different. Perhaps you thought you only had an average year when in fact your competitors were much worse off and you were the stellar hotel in the area. Or vice versa.

On conclusion, hotel price control/income management strategy may bring below these benefits to any hotels as below, they may include as below:

1. Less costly errors

While larger hotels might be able to hide or easily overcome a pricing mistake, smaller hotels have less margin for error. An incorrect price at a small hotel will have a bigger impact on ADR and RevPAR.

2. Get more revenue out of every room

With fewer rooms, maximising the rate for each room becomes more critical. The data your technology provides will help you understand who you should be targeting and when. What will be the most valuable demand for you? For example, do you offer rates for group business? Do you offer discounts for long stays?

3. Know your competitors better

To get your own pricing strategy right, you need to know what your immediate competitors are doing. With a pricing intelligence tool you can get an instant all-in-one overview of your competitors rate activity, meaning you can concentrate on why they are adjusting and how/if you should respond.

4. It makes your hotel 'bigger'

Large, branded hotels will already have an RMS in place – and dedicated revenue managers to manage them – and while independent hotels may not be able to afford a robust solution, pricing intelligence tools are an affordable substitute. These use the data and its own algorithms to carry out a real-time analysis of the state of the market, and of demand, in order to calculate ideal room rates. Increasing your data visibility and analysis capabilities gives you more ammunition to compete with large hotel groups who are able to devote full-time staff to revenue management.

5. Manage your time efficiently

Automated market intelligence will allow you to instantly access and act upon pricing data. Knowing when the market will be an easy sell-out or in a quiet period will not only enable you to optimise rates, but with a dependable forecast, you can organise your staff more effectively and improve the guest experience.

6. You can be proactive

The more data you have access to, the less reactive you'll be. Rather than reacting to your competitors all the time, you'll better understand demand, make your own projections, and set intelligent rates.

7. Understand your guests better

A RMS can tell you more about customer behaviour and allow you to attract more bookings. For example, do guests prefer it when your rate applies to every night of their stay, or will they accept varying rates, or do they prefer a total stay price?

8. Your data will come from a single source

Instead of combing through your own data, and then individually doing the same for competitors, an RMS will collate everything for you in one place. Depending on your system, you can do this for up to 15 competitors. If you are a smaller hotel that is new to revenue management strategies, doing everything manually might have you tearing your hair out.

Hence, any hotels can not neglect to consider how to

implement price and income management strategy in order to achieve the highest profit aim.

THREE

HOTEL ROOM LIVING SERVICE CONSUMER PSYCHOLOGICAL FACTORS

What are some noticeable hotel service trends in the industry ?

Travellers of today are diverse and want to stay in a place which lets them live out their individuality. They want a hotel which adapts to them, not the other way around. The quest for individualised experiences sets them apart from older generations and has created a challenge for many hoteliers. Guests expect convenience, simplicity and the same instant gratification they enjoy in other areas of their lives. However, hotel and resort staff face the daunting task of handling an endless array of guest issues with a limited team. No matter how well trained front desk staff might be, there are always occasions where long lines form and waiting guests become frustrated. Even a five-minute wait in a check-in line can result in a 50% reduction in guest satisfaction scores. Moreover, guests have become accustomed to the Airbnbs of the world where everything offered to them is extremely relevant and guest has the option to tweak the experience themselves. A similar trend is seen among major hotel chains, where they are using loyalty solutions to promote offers and services based on the guests' preferences and guests have the ability to check-in using mobile. Independent hotels are slowly but steadily starting to embrace such solutions. Personalisation of guest service is no longer a trend, but an obligation for hotels. For example, traditional check-in times were designed for a guest that no longer exists. With long haul travel now very much mainstream, 40% of guests are either arriving on flights before 7AM or leaving on flights that take off after 6PM. Tailoring check-in/check out times to your guest's travel plans is the next battleground of personalisation."

What's the power of automation for hotels and guests?

By combining powerful segmentation with a high-conversion platform, upselling can really help deliver the five R's of revenue management: Selling the right room on the right channel to the right customer at the right time at the right price. Using segmentation properly allows you to target and market to a variety of potential buyers with varying needs, behaviors and budgets. Doing this well will provide you data needed to understand the success of your current revenue strategies and adjust them to maximise your topline in the future. Software providers can take most of that work off your hands. Setting up your segments is done in a matter of minutes, and the software handles the rest, like making sure the segments you choose are offered attractive deals in automatically sent emails."

Can AI platforms or chatbots raise travellers living hotel room choice need ?

Artificial Intelligence (AI) platforms or chatbots can be used to answer simple guest questions and requests freeing up hotel staff to focus on the most complicated guest issues. With mobile keys, bluetooth technology allows mobile devices to communicate directly with the door lock on a guest room.Automation technology can also be leveraged to enhance communication between the hotel staff and guest. Platforms like ours at OpenKey also gives hotels the ability to offer mobile dining, valet requests, concierge, and other guest services – in addition to a digital key – from a mobile app.

I believe that AI technology can boost your hotel brand perception. Automating guest communication opens up a tremendous potential for the hotel. Typically pre-arrival or confirmation emails have been seen as just a system-generated message verifying that a reservation has been made. But this is the first time guest hears about you. "Wouldn't it be nice, if you could delight the guest with a warm greeting, in their own language, with offers that are specific to their profile or segment? With proper tools, this can be easily achieved. For exmaple, if a guest booked a standard room, the system may automatically offer the deluxe room. Or if the airport is far away, offer them a fully arranged taxi service. If targeted properly, upsell and cross-sell efforts can significantly improve guest satisfaction as offers are more relevant. When should you send the offer and who should you send it to? Hotels often send their upsell offers too early when the pain point the hotel is looking to solve is not front of mind for the guest. How should you change your offer depending on the nature of the guest? We'll change how we target and what we offer guests depending on nationality and travel time.

Moreover, AI technology is helping hotels to be more efficient. From the perspective of some hotels which apply AI technology, these hotels look to elevate their service, mobile technology will help us deliver a simplified and efficient guest experience. Today's traveller wants to save time and enjoy their travel, not wait in check-in lines. These hotels could help their customers can be happier about adding a tech solution that will ultimately benefit to their per booking hotel rooms service before they catch pair planes to arrive their country. So, they do not need to spend much time to find the best suitable hotel to live when the hotel can apply AI technology to help them to make hotel choice decision. For example, hoteliers are slowly beginning to understand that technology is not here to replace the human touch but to complement it. Historically guest-facing technology was seen as a toy they can live without. But more and more guests expect these types of convenience services and hotels are realising, this is the new norm. Most guests are not overly expressive about their wants and needs. This means, without tech, it will become extremely difficult to deliver superior guest experience.

How important is connectivity for hoteliers and the platforms they use? As a minimum we need the reservation data from hotel guests, which can be gleaned from the PMS, channel manager, or OTA. So it's important these systems are able to integrate easily with each other. Connectivity is the most important influential factor: Without it any lacking AI technological communication assistance hotels can't automate their services for their clients, which means adding manual work to the hotel's front desk, which simply doesn't work. The ability for technology to continue to help hotels run their businesses, hinges on the providers ability to connect into the hotel's tech stack. Moreover, hoteliers completely understand the pivotal role of tech, but their hands have been tied by the lack of connectivity offered by their incumbent technology systems.

On conclusion, hotel management is about overseeing every operation of the property. This requires knowledge of distribution strategy, finance, customer service, staff management, marketing, and more. Effective inventory management for hotels involves both creating and managing demand, and maximising returns. Revenue management is another huge part of managing your hotel. How do you get more money coming in and achieve business goals?

In the hospitality industry almost everything revolves around the customer, and they're the quickest party to point out any flaws. Good management eliminates as many mistakes as possible. Hotel management sometimes also requires the management of a restaurant. Turn your hotel restaurant into a premium dining experience that focuses on the whole package including the food, lighting, music, decor, and wine lists. This way, your restaurant won't only be the bait to bring new customers in, but also an incentive for current guests to return when they revisit the area.

Similar to search engines such as Google, OTAs have their own algorithms for how your property will rank, meaning you need to pay close attention to how you build your profile on them. Fighting food waste at your hotel goes beyond feeding people and helping the environment – it also improves your property's bottom line. Reporting on performance is essential to hotel management. You need to collect and analyse accurate data regularly to see where things are working, and what you need to improve on. Hotel management software is technology that allows hotel operators and owners to streamline their administrative tasks while also increasing their bookings in both the short- and long-term. Managing a hotel isn't all about managing the physical property, it's also about managing intangible things like reputation. There are many apps in the market to help with everyday challenges. Organised teams get more done and having everything under control also gives you a better grip on the overall success of the business.

● How and why hotel managers need to attempt to predict customer booking hotel room behavior or booking hotel room need psychology?

Any hotel management ought need to learn how to predict hotel entertainment consumer individual need in order to attract consumer living choice or increase consumers number easily. I assume that if the hotel can provide the room living service can let any hotel consumers to feel such ad themselves homes feeling. It will influence them to live longer time to stay in the hotel (prolonging hotel room booking days) in the hotel because they can feel themselves homes living feeling. How can make hotel room booking consumers to feel the hotel rooms are such as their homes living feeling? it is one interesting question to discuss. I shall explain as below;

Building hotel living holiday leisure feeling, this factor is very important to influence hotel living consumers to make final extending proplonging living consumers to make final extending or prolonging living days in the hotel. Holidays, by definition , are non-working times, an extended period of anticipated recreation, especially away from home, they can be days of festivity when no work is done. The prolem and opportunity for hotel living entertainment service providers, is that when hotel living customers are on holiday, or at leisure. Hotels need to give a chance of getting away from living holidays, new changing the batteries and for some a change of holiday living of entertainment lifestyle. Hence, if the hotel can let all customers to feel home comfortable living feeling to enjoy their one part of entertainment activity in the whole journeys. The hotel may persuade any one customer (hotel room living customers to prolong any one customer (hotel room living customers to prolong living days in the hotel).

Will the broad framework of leisure defined as time, there are many variations. In general, defining leisure as the time when someone is not working primarrily for money. So, if the hotel room living customer can feel that he/she spends the booking room living fee is value to choose the hotel room to live. The hotel room is such as unoccupied time or free time in whose journey time. Due to he/she feels that this living hotel room time is whose entertainment time. It is essential, then this unoccupied time may persuade him/her to prolong booking hotel room living time in the hotel. For example, he planned to stay 5 days in the hotel, but because he/she feels that the hotel can provide entertainment activities time to attract him/her to stay longer time in the hotel, e.g. gym sport facilities are very attractive sport playing entertainment or hotel restaurant can provide good taste food eating time in special dinner, breakfast, lunch time or swimming pool is beautiful design and large size and it can let him/her to feel actual natural beach environment feeling. Then, any one these extra entertainment facilities or services factors may influence any one customer to spend extending living time in the hotel. Such as this cause, this hotel living customer may feel need to live more two to three days, even more days in this hotel. Hence, hotel leisure as time psychological factor is also important to influence any one hotel room living customer to influence any one hotel oom living consumer to make extending living time decision easily, when they feel this hotel has themselves homes feeling.

Kraus & Bates (1975) add experiencing to the activity. Recreation consists of activities or experiences with are carried on volutarily in leisure time. They are chosen by participants, either for pleasure or to satisfy certain personal needs when provided as part of organized community programs, creation must be designed to achieve constructive goals.

Hence, if the hotel can consist any recreation actvities or experiences to let any one hotel living customer to enjoy to live when are carried on voluntarily in their leisure time. They can choose any kinds of leisure activities to play and live in the hotel, if the hotel any one kind of leisure activity can satisfy their leisure needs. Then, the hotel's any kind of leisure activity can achieve constructive goals to persuade any one hotel room living consumer likes to spend extra money to enjoy any kinds of hotel leisure facilties, instead of spending extra hotel room living expenditure to proplong hotel time in the hotel. Hence, it seems that whether the hotel can provide attractive leisure facilities to let consumers to relationship to influence they their long living or staying time in the hotel.

When asked what were the three most important factors in the development of hotel. Thus equality applied to most leisure facilities ideally, a public transport location may influence any one hotel room customer to choose which hotel location is the nearest to public transport in order to pay cheap transport fee to catch the public transport. This is one low transport fee cost factor to influence the potential hotel room customer choice.

Hence, any hotel's location will be chosen to build to near many public transport tools, e.g. buses, underground trains, taxis, trains station locations. It aims to attract the hotel room booking potential customers can pay cheap public transport fee to arrive their hotel conveniently. They do not need to spend long walking time to arrive their hotels after they catch any one kind of public transport tool to arrive their hotel destinations. Moreover, they do not need to spend long time to find where the hotel locates when they leave the bus stop. So, geographical location factor will be another main factor to influence hotel consumer choices.

The model is based on comparing demand and supply economc theory:

1. identifying where hotel demand is located, whether and to what extent, hotel rooms number demand exceeds hotel rooms number supply in the geographical area and whether , and where, the city has much land to provide space capacity to permit to build hotels number exists in the geographical area in the city.

2. Moreover, local demand is measured on the basis of the number of hotel visits per week in peack period for any hotel room needs determined by:

The total number of travelling visitors in the month rate , the demand rate, the proportion of residents who want to book room to live in the hotel, instead of overseas travelling visitors, the desired frequency of visits, how often overseas travellers want to visit the country and the proportation of visits which arise in the normal peiods per month, such as christmas, New Year etc. public holidays.

So, all of these hotel visitors public transport fee cheap demand number and hotel geographical locations, hotel entertainment facilities , hotel comfortable living feeling, hotel safety, hotel food taste, public holiday and visitor individual travelling need, air ticket price main factors which will influence any one hotel's room demand and supply number absolutely in behavioral economic theory view, instead of hotel environment and service performance basic element factor.

On conclusion, all of these any one element may influence any one hotel customers numner increases or decreases absolutely. Hence, any one hotel management can not neglect to learn how to implement their hotel management strategies effectively.

ref.

Kraus , R. & Batees , B. (1975). Creation leadership and supervision, W.B. Saunders, philadelphia, P.A.

How to supervise teams in hospitality industry

Any hotels need effective supervisors to supervise their teams in different department in order to raise service efficiency. How to supervise teams which is one important question to any hotels? I shall attempt to explain as below:

In hospitaloty industry, alomst everything depends on the psycical labour of many hours (non-managerial workers), waiters, mix drinks, wash dishes, checkquests, clean room, carry bags, mop floors, even security etc. All of these teams must need a supervisor to manage their make products and/or perform services. The human resources for personnel, and training departments are example of staffs who advise line departments, such as the food and beverage department on matters including hiring, disciplining and training.

In general, supervisor responsibility may include: achieving or exceeding the expected results, on time and on budget, planning or determining priorities. Organizing (scheduling), motivating (creative a positive work environment), controlling (monitoring and taking corrective action if mistakes are outside acceptable limits), communicating effectively.

In the reality, in a hotel you may have 5,000 minimum customers are day. You deal with your supervisors. You deal with your subordinates, and you deal with your guests, all coming at you from different directons. Salepeople , deliveries, inspectors, customer complaints and applicants . You jobs interrupt you. So , you are likely to have only a few seconds available when you make many important decisons.

You will feel bus to deal any of either above, these matters every day. Hence, in effective hotel organization, it needs have effective scientific management, it incudes these elements: Standardization, of work procedures, tool and conditions of work through design of work methods by specialists, careful selection of competent people, after training, and elimination of these (traineers) who could not or would not perform, complete and constant overseeing of the work, with total obedience from the worker' incenive pay for meeting the fair day for meeting the fair day's work standard, the worker's share of the increased productivity.

How to innovate hotel tasks to be work simplification or searching for the best way of performance tasks ? Supervisors can use time-and-motion study techniques, developing ways of simplifying tasks than often doubled or triples what a worker would do. This methods and principles had a great impact in food service kitchen, where work simplification techniques have been explored widely adopted. This methods ewere adopted although the idea that have hotel worker should share in the benefits of increased productivity seldom went along with the rest of the system. For example, in hotel kitcehen department , every cooking steep is systematized, and the cooker, dish cleaner is simply taught to run the kitchen dish cleaning machines, cooking machines follow the rules, and speak given phrases. When the kitchen bell rings, the cooker turns the hamburgers on dispenser one time, where is no room for deviation.

How a supervisor can build a positive work climate in his/her hotel department ? He/She needs to know his/her employee expectation and need. You may wonder whethet their performance will meet your expectation, and you may have some plans for improving productivity. But you may not realize that what there people expect from you and how you meet their expectations may have as much to do with their performance as your expectation of them. However, your staffs also expect you to be qualified to supervise. First, they want you to have worked in the area in which you are supervising: a hotel, room, a hotel kitchen, a hotel restaurant, lowing into a big motel from a job in a budget motel, you may also improve yourself. Your staffs want to feel that you understand the operation well and appreciate the work , they are doing. They want to feel that they and their jobs are in good hands, that you are truly capable of directing their work.

- Behavior modification supervising strategy

Behavior modification explains a newer method for improving performance. It explains all behavior is a function of its consequences; people behave as they do because of positive or negative consequences to them. If the consequences are positive, they will trend to repeat the behaviors, if they are negative, they will trend not to . Hence, if you are hotel kitchen cookers their supervisor, you need to give praise , or appreciation to the cookers , whose cooking skills can be improved when they can cook good taste foods ro satisfy hotel restaurant customer individual eatting feeling. Every time, you need to give praise to the excellent cooker's cooking performance. Then, his/her cooking skills will be improved , due to your praise. It is possible that he/she feels salary will be increased by your praise. Otherwise, when you feel the cooker's cooking skill is worse and your cookers their cooking foods taste are also worse and they can not satisy your cookers their customers' eatting taste needs often. Then , you ought not punish or blam to let him/her by your oral blaming or pubishment threat (without salary increasing threat). Consequently, his /her cooking skill can not be improved, even worse. You ought attempt to help him/her to find whether which aspects of cooking skills , he/she is felt to need to learn how to improve hir/her cooking skill to be better, and you ought teach him/her how to cool the kinds of food to be better taste. Consequently, his/her cooking skill will be improved by your teaching and patience excuse attitude.

- How to design clear job analysis?

Any one hotel team ought need have clear job analysis to let their departments supervisors and staffs to know whether what aspects of tasks , they need to do in order to achieve actual work performance improvement. For example, sever job units example, it may include: Stock service station, set tables, great quests, explain menu to customers, take food and beverage orders and complete guest check, pick up order and complete plate preparation, serve food, recommand wines and serve them, total and present check, perform side work, operate equipment , meet dress and grooming stantards, observe sanitation procedures and requirements, maintain good customer relations, and desired check arrange.

Hence, any one hotel restaurant server can know whether how they require the setting standards, training and evaluation jst as the actual work sequences do. Such units appears in ither jobs as well , and the same standards will apply in each case in the hotel any departments performance standards from the heart of the job description and they describe the what, how to and how wells of a job.

1. What the employee is to do?
2. How it is to be done?
3. To what extent it is to be done?

It means that any hotel department staffs and supervisors they need to know concern their job requirement such as : How much, how well, how soon. For example, " one waitor or waitress job at acertain restaurant. The server will take food and beverage orders for up to five tables with 100 % accuracy, using standard house procedures." It is the hotel restaurant waitor/waitress general job standard acceptance level.

Hence, waitor/waitress supervisor can folle this guideline to know how to supervise his/her staffs and evaluate whose job performance in the hotel restaurant.

On conclusion, due to hotel is one service industry, any hotel's different department effective supervising management, they need have good job standard, training and fair evaluation performance system, fair compensation and pubishment system, instead of the department supervisor whose supervising effort or ability whether is proficient or worse in order to influence whose team serving performance effectively and efficiently . However, any organization itself management team and supervising team will need have good communicating technique in order to let any department supervisor knows how to supervise his/her team effectively in order to achieve improvement service performance aim.

www.ingramcontent.com/pod-product-compliance
Ingram Content Group UK Ltd.
Pitfield, Milton Keynes, MK11 3LW, UK
UKHW040009200726
13854UKWH00001B/115

9 798887 339474